CATALYTIC QUOTES

BORGO PRESS BOOKS BY WILLIAM MALTESE:

Anal Cousins: Case Studies in Variant Sexual Practices
Blood-Red Resolution: Being Excerpts from the Crypto-Coded Files of the United Courier Service
Catalytic Quotes (Some Heard Through a Time Warp)
Emerald-Silk Intrigue
The Fag Is Not for Burning: A Mystery Novel
From This Beloved Hour
Gerun, the Heretic: Being Excerpts from the Clan-Missionary Chronicles
The Gomorrha Conjurations
Heart on Fire: A Romance
Jungle Quest Intrigue
Love's Emerald Flame
Love's Golden Spell
Moonstone Intrigue
Moonstone Murders: The Movie Script
Slaves
A Slip to Die for: A Stud Draqual Mystery
Summer Sweat: An Erotic Anthology
SS & M: Being Excerpts from the Nazi Death-Head Files
When Summer Comes
Young Cruisers

FOR OTHER PRESSES:

Beyond Machu
Bond-Shattering
The Brentridge Gold: The Pleiades Portals Series
Circusex: A One-Hand Read®
A Conspiracy of Ravens: A One-Hand Read®
Diary of a Hustler
Dog on a Surfboard and Other Adventures
Goldsands
Slovakian Boy
SS Mann Hunt
Thai Died: A Stud Draqual Mystery

CATALYTIC QUOTES
(Some Heard Through a Time Warp)

One Music- History- Literary- and Trivia-Buff's Pure Conjecture on the Seemingly Sometimes Idiosyncratic Transmigration of the Creative Muse

WILLIAM MALTESE

BORGO PRESS

CATALYTIC QUOTES

Copyright © 2008 by William Maltese.
All rights reserved.

No part of this book may be reproduced in any form
without the expressed written consent
of the author and publisher.
Printed in the United States of America

www.wildsidepress.com

FIRST EDITION

PROLOGUE

CATALYTIC: Causing significant reaction.

QUOTES: Written for another with credit acknowledgements.

(SOME: A certain amount.

HEARD: Perceived.

THROUGH: Movement into at one side and out at another.

A TIME WARP: An anomaly or discontinuity held to occur in time progression**).**

PROLOGUE

HANK AARON to WILLIAM GOLDING:
"Yep. Me. The Lord of the Flies."

HANK AARON to ELVIS PRESLEY:
"You've got to learn to *swing* from the hip."

LEON ABBOT to ETHEL MERMAN:
"We're looking for a few good people to work on the stage."

THE ABDOMINABLE SNOWMAN to DOCTOR PHIBES:
"I'm abominable?! You're the one who's abominable!"

ACE to JOHN HOLMES:
"How long?"

ADAM to FOUR TOPS:
"I was always telling Eve — 'Ain't no woman like the one I've got.'"

ADAM to NOEL LANGLEY:
"When I really get perturbed at her, I call her by her full name."

ADAM to JOSEPH L. MANKIEWICZ:
"Oh, I couldn't tell you all about Eve, but I'm putting it in my book."

ADAM to BARRY MC GUIRE:
"After that business in the garden, with the apple, and all the resulting havoc, my private nickname for her became 'Eve of Destruction'."

ADAM to THE OSMONDS:
"I don't have to tell you the havoc that resulted from that one bad apple."

ALADDIN to STEPPENWOLF:
"Personally, I always found a magic-carpet ride preferable to any tour bus."

ALADDIN to STEVIE WONDER:
"*I wish* can be two pretty powerful words when you've just summoned genie from his bottle."

EDWIN EUGENE ALDRIN, JR. to BILLY PRESTON:
"No doubt about my having been part of the space race."

MUHAMMAD ALI to MICKEY FINN:
"Talk about a knock-out."

MUHAMMAD ALI to ANDY GIBB:
"I don't care what it looks like, it's shadow *boxing*."

MUHAMMAD ALI to JIMMY HATLO:
"Why, I'll be just fine with the help of a little iodine."

MUHAMMAD ALI to GENE MC DANIELS:
"Yes. Somewhere, back in my adolescence, I guess you could say I was one-hundred pounds of Clay."

MUHAMMAD ALI to HARRY TUGEND:
"Yes, I was caught in the draft, but did I get the shaft, and end up in Vietnam, killed by a bomb?"

ALL THE KINGS MEN to PABLO PICASSO:
"Hell, no we don't have a photo of Mr. Dumpty, but we're sure he'll appreciate whatever we can do."

DON AMECHE to SUSO CHECCHI D'AMICO and ALBA DE CESPEDES:
"Look guys, I'm really flattered that you named your movie after me, but I'm really afraid I'm going to have to pass on this one."

JAY ANSON to XAVIERA HOLLANDER:
"I know you're concerned about this whore moving in on your Amityville business, but just what makes you think there's a book in it?"

MARIE ANTOINETTE to LES BAXTER:
"So what that there are poor people of Paris? There are poor people of Rome, and poor people of Moscow, and poor people of The Bronx."

MARIE ANTOINETTE to BETTY CROCKER:
"Let them eat cake."

MARIE ANTOINETTE to FRANCO BRUSATI, IAIA FIASTRI, and NINO MANFREDI:
"Let them eat bread and chocolate!"

MARIE ANTOINETTE to THE KINGSMEN:
"Louis, Louis. That's all I ever hear. Doesn't anyone want to know what I think about anything?

MARCUS ANTONIUS to VINCENT VAN GOGH:
"Friends, Romans, countrymen, lend me your ear."

ADRIADNE to LINDA RONSTADT:
"The secret of the Labyrinth? As I told Theseus, 'It's so easy to figure out if you just trail a simple string behind you.'"

ARISTOTLE to MASON WILLIAMS:
"Excuse, please. Must be something I ate."

ROSEANNE (BARR) ARNOLD to THE FOUR SEASONS:
"So, whenever I got weepy, mom would always say, 'Come on, Roseanne, big girls don't cry.'"

ROSEANNE (BARR) ARNOLD to THE HUMAN LEAGUE:
"So, I said to Warren Beatty — 'I don't understand. Don't you want me?'"

ART TEACHER to GEORGES SEURAT:
"Try a little harder to get the point, Georges."

JEAN ARTHUR to ALBERT PAYSON TERHUNE:
"My opinion of Alan Ladd? A dog as far as an actor."

KING ARTHUR to GEORGE BENSON
"Give me the knight who offended, and I'll personally see he's punished."

KING ARTHUR to MICHAEL HOGAN
"Of course, I would have liked some Arabian knights, but there's the religious thing."

KING ARTHUR to THE EAGLES
"Take a look. One of these knights is going to betray me."

KING ARTHUR to THE MOODY BLUES
"Talk about a drag ball, I never saw so many knights in white satin."

ARTHUR ASHE to BRIGHAM YOUNG:
"Love fifteen!"

ASSOCIATE OF SIR WILLIAM HERSCHEL to SIR WILLIAM HERSCHEL:
"I'm telling you, Bill, name that planet after your butt, and you'll make an ass of yourself."

ATTILA THE HUN to KURT WEILL:
"If you must know the truth, I wouldn't give more than three cents for any opera."

JOHN JAMES AUDUBON to TIPPI HEDREN:
"You're going to the birds."

JOHN AUDUBON to D.H. LAWRENCE:
"Yep. They banded this rook in Boston, and it's been soaring ever since."

JEAN AUEL to H.H. MUNRO:
"The chronicles of Clovis man would make interesting reading, don't you think? I mean, for one, the how of their fantastic spear- and arrowheads."

BACCHUS to PHILIPPE DE MORNAY:
"I can tell you're a man who likes his sauce."

BACCHUS to JAMES WHITCOMB RILEY:
"When has Robert Frost had too much to drink? Well, I could only tell for sure once. At the Halloween party when he was on the pumpkin."

JOHANN SEBASTIAN BACH to LAWRENCE DURRELL:
"After the Brandenburg concertos, I was going to go for an Alexandria quartet, but it never happened."

KARL BAEDEKER to THE 1910 FRUITGUM COMPANY:
"How many did I see? One. Two. Three red-light districts, starting with the one in Amsterdam."

JAMES ADDISON BAKER to VIRGINIA WOOLF:
"So, I told the butcher and the candlestick maker, 'You want to get this tub to shore, you'd better look to the lighthouse.'"

JIM BAKKER to BILLY PRESTON AND SYREETA:
"It's true. With you, I'm born again."

JAMES BAKKER to HERMAN'S HERMITS:
"Listen, people, I have sinned."

TAMMY FAYE BAKKER to WILLIAM K. HOWARD:
"I was really worried that the only way Jim and I would end up in heaven was through the back door."

TAMMY FAYE BAKKER to THE MONKEES:
"No matter what Jim may or may not have done … no matter what people think I may or may not have done … as God is my witness, my faith was not been shaken. Truly, I'm a believer!"

ROCKY BALBOA to JAMES LICK:
"Hey, man? Want you should see stars?"

JAMES BALDWIN to LAWRENCE WELK:
"You know what Truman Capote said, right there at that party, in front of everyone? 'James, you are the black hole of Calcutta!' The bitch!"

CAT BALLOU to VERDI:
"I eat fish every Friday and can't sing praises high enough."

BAMBI to STEPHANE MALLARME:
"But you promised this afternoon would be all mine."

BARBIE to JACQUELINE SUSANN:
"Couldn't you write something about us valley girls?"

PT. BARNUM to Dracula:
"There's one of you guys born every minute."

RED BARON to BILLY WILDER:
"I was hunting in Africa and fell into this hole someone dug for lions. More than a few American flyers came to wish I had never climbed out."

SIDNEY BIDDLE BARROWS to ZOE AKINS, DORIS ANDERSON, GOUVERNEUR MORRIS:
"You have it all wrong. I, personally, was never anybody's woman. Mine was purely a managerial capacity."

SIDNEY BIDDLE BARROWS to BRUCE MANNING and FELIX JACKSON:
"Look guys, you want a specific girl, it's always preferable to call ahead and make an appointment."

SIDNEY BIDDLE BARROWS to ALAN MELVILLE:
"I guess my mistake was thinking only of the customers. You know, 'As long as they're happy, I'm doing great.' Trouble with that was how I'd left the cops out of the equation."

SIDNEY BIDDLE BARROWS to MORDECAI RICHLER:
"I had to tell this Duddy Kravitz that I didn't care who gave him my address, there was no way I could offer him any kind of apprenticeship."

SIDNEY BIDDLE BARROWS to GALE STORM:
"I must insist you keep it down in there. I run a respectable establishment, and I hear you knockin'."

SIDNEY BIDDLE BARROWS to THE FOUR LADS:
"Standing on the corner was never my thing."

SIDNEY BIDDLE BARROWS to GENE TOWNE and WILLIAM CONSELMAN:
"I would have considered it very unprofessional, from my purely managerial capacity, to mix business and pleasure. Most of my girls, too, managed to keep the two quite separate."

HALL BARTLETT to BILLY PRESTON:
"Okay, here are the clues. Arthur Hailey did the teleplay. It's a two-word title, second word 'Hour'. Last clue— nothing from nothing."

NORMAN BATES to MAXIM GORKY:
"Mother was something else again."

BATMAN to THE STEVE MILLER BAND:
"Rumor is you have the Joker."

SAMMY BAUGH to FRANK CARNEY:
"Hut!"

LYMAN BAUM to AMERICA:
"I've got a little girl from Kansas. Her dog. A friendly lion. A scarecrow. Can you think of anyone or anything I'm missing?"

LYMAN BAUM to PABLO NERUDA:
"It's about this girl from Kansas, a scarecrow, and a tin man, all headed off to the splendid city where the wizard lives."

JIM BEAM to D.W. GRIFFITH and FRANK E. WOODS:
"Eighteen-forty-six. A year Johnny Walker and I remember very well. 'Twas the year Carry Nation was born. And that, my friend, was the birth of a Nation we wished had never occurred."

WARREN BEATTY to ALLEN DRURY:
"I tell you, they gave their advice and consent. Ask Rob Lowe if you don't believe me."

CATALYTIC QUOTES 13

WARREN BEATTY to HERMAN'S HERMITS:
"I walked right up and said, 'Mrs. Brown, you have a lovely daughter.' Turns out, Georgia Brown is a stage name. What's more, she's never even heard of Murphy."

WARREN BEATTY to HAROLD MEDFORD and SAMUEL FULLER:
"They can say what they want, but there was never a Capetown affair."

WARREN BEATTY to THOMAS PAINE:
"That's right, I confess. I got her pregnant. Had I used a rubber, I wouldn't have."

WARREN BEATTY to OSCAR SAUL:
"How can I possibly tell you about my affair in Trinidad when I've never even been there? Why not talk to Anatol, Annabel, Cellini, Martha, Susan, even Dobie Gillis? Now, their affairs are ten times more film-worthy than mine."

WARREN BEATTY to AMII STEWART:
"No! I definitely did not knock up Wood. Oh, I'm sorry. You're talking knock on *wood*. I thought you were dredging up my affair with Natalie."

WARREN BEATTY to DEREK TWIST:
"Would you believe that it's all over the town that Annette Bening is having our baby?"

WARREN BEATTY to EDMUND WARD:
"I categorically deny having had an Amsterdam affair with any Hollander."

THOMAS A. BECKET to GEOFFREY CHAUCER:
"Have I got tales to tell."

THOMAS A. BECKET to T.S. ELIOT:
"Do you like that? Do you? If you do, that's okay. A lot of people do. However, you know what I think? I think Bach, playing that racket, is getting away with murder in the cathedral."

LAWRENCE BEESLY to ROY CRANE:
"I said, 'Captain, easy it may be, but no way am I steering the *Titanic* through those ice flows.'"

PAT BENATOR to AIR SUPPLY and LIONEL RICHIE:
"You know how love is a battlefield a lot of the time? Well, all night long … all night … with Claude Rains, is like making love out of nothing at all."

ANNETTE BENING to FREDDIE AND THE DREAMERS:
"Can you believe it? So, I said — 'What do you mean, Mr. Warren Beatty, that I didn't tell you I was pregnant? I'm telling you now.'"

ANNETTE BENING to EUGENE O'NEIL:
"I tell you, Warren Beatty can experience desire anywhere. In a closet. On the kitchen table. Under the elms."

ANNETTE BENING to THE BEATLES:
"Yes, Warren wanted to make love on the long and winding road."

ANNETTE BENING to THE DRIFTERS:
"Yes, Warren wanted to do it under the boardwalk."

ANNETTE BENING to THE DRIFTERS:
"Yes, Warren even wanted to do it up on the roof."

ANNETTE BENING to THE MOMENTS:
"Yes, Warren wanted to make love on a two-way street, too."

ANNETTE BENING to THE NEW VAUDEVILLE BAND:
"Please do me a favor and don't even suggest to Warren that we visit Winchester Cathedral."

ANNETTE BENING to BOBBY VEE:
"So, I said to Warren — 'Not only am I going to have it, but I expect you to take good care of my baby.'"

JAMES GORDON BENNETT to RALPH LAUREN:
"You could be a real winner in polo."

MILTON BERLE to THE COMMODORES:
"Guys, I've dressed in drag so many times that saying I was only three times a lady would be gross underestimation."

LEONARD BERSTEIN to THE SUPREMES:
"Isn't that Beethoven's fifth glass of champagne?"

BIG BAD WOLF to ALFRED NOBEL:
"I'm going to blow your house down."

BIG BAD WOLF to SAM THE SHAM AND THE PHARAOHS:
"No doubt about it. I was out to get Lil' Red Ridinghood, and if that meant dressing in drag to do it, then I was prepared to play granny."

BIG BAD WOLF to THE SENSATIONS:
"So, I said to those little pigs — 'Let me in, or I'll huff and I'll puff, and I'll blow your house in!'"

BILL HALEY AND HIS COMETS to EUGENE LING:
"Rock Hudson was so drunk, he asked us what time it was, every hour on the hour. We spent the whole time, between midnight and dawn, saying — 'One o'clock, two o'clock, three o'clock, Rock. Four o'clock, five o'clock, six o'clock, Rock.'"

BILLY THE KID to CHARLES SCHULZ:
"Draw!"

KAREN BLACK to THREE DOG NIGHT:
"Can't you just picture me and Betty White together?"

BEN BLUE to DOROTHY MOORE:
"Sure, there are times when I get emotional. Invariably, though, there is someone to say, 'Lookin' Misty, Blue?' And, I usually snap right out of it."

BLUE IMAGE to JEAN-LUC PICARD:
"Ride, Captain, ride!"

JAMES BOND to WILLIAM J. LAMBERT III, WILLIAM BOWERS, SHELDON REYNOLDS, and GIUSEPPE RAMATI:
"It was assignment Grey Area, and it took me to Paris to kill a member of the Assisi Underground."

JAMES BOND to RIVERS:
"Just what exactly did you want to know about being a secret agent, man?"

JAMES BOND to MARTY ROBBINS:
"So, I asked 'M' just how I'm supposed to recognize this guy. He says, 'Easy. It's a hockey game, isn't it? He'll be the only one in a white sport coat and a pink carnation.'"

JAMES BOND to THEODORE N. VAIL:
"I've got your number."

JAMES BOND to EDMUND WILSON:
"I knew I'd committed a major blunder when they threatened to send me to the Finland station."

JAMES BOND to BILL WITHERS:
"So, I came right out and told the Marquis de Sade — 'Don't even, for a minute, think either you, or Leopold von Sacher-Masoch, is going to use me.'"

WILLIAM BONNEY to QUEEN:
"Damn right, just about every time I draw, another one bites the dust."

WILLIAM BONNEY to THE EAGLES:
"So, I'm not in Hollywood a week before Sue Mengers asks about the new kid in town. That's how hot I am."

BONNIE AND CLYDE to THE CAPTAIN AND TENNILLE:
"Through good times and bad, we've never had any doubts that love will keep us together. Not to mention the cash from the bank robberies."

SONNY BONO to THE ASSOCIATION:
"Cher is her own woman. I'll give her that much."

DEBBY BOONE to THOMAS ALVA EDISON:
"You light up my life."

GAIL BORDEN to ANNE FRANK:
"There's nothing to give people more satisfaction than a really good dairy."

GAIL BORDEN to ELVIS PRESLEY:
"So, I'm at this guy-from-our-lab's house, and I accidentally tip this beaker of gunk all over these rock-and-roll publicity stills that he collects. Wouldn't you know, most of the mess ends up stuck on you?!"

JAMES BOWIE to GERALD DRAYSON ADAMS and GEOFFREY HOMES:
"Now, this gentlemen, is the knife I call, 'The Big Steel'."

DAVID BOWIE to IRENE CARA:
"So, I said to Annie Lennox, 'Let's dance the flashdance.' What a feeling! She told me, 'Sweet dreams are made of this.' I agreed."

THOMAS BRADLEY to GARY LARSON:
"You think strange things go down here, you should try the far side of town."

MARLON BRANDO to THE CRYSTALS:
"I know *I* have that kind of reputation, but as far as I'm concerned, James Dean — *he's* a rebel."

NORMAN BRINKER to DRACULA:
"You'll like my steaks."

DOCTOR JOYCE BROTHERS to THE BEATLES:
"I had her problem figured out from the start. 'Medusa,' I diagnosed, 'all you need is love — and, of course, a new hairdo.'"

FARMER BROWN to D.H. LAWRENCE:
"It was my argument that a man couldn't have enough sons. But wouldn't you know, Casanova jumped right in with 'and lovers'."

JOHN BROWN to JAMES BROWN:
"Hey, bro!"

LEROY BROWN to DONNA SUMMER:
"So, I told that band of high-school cheerleaders, 'Better watch out, because I'm bad, bad, and I do mean bad, girls.'"

WILLIAM BUCKLEY to BOBBY VINTON:
"On tonight's program, I'm going to have Ben Blue discuss the new movie, 'Blue,' by director Silvio Narizzano."

BUDDHA to LORD NELSON:
"Concentrate on your navel."

BULLWINKLE to SYLVESTER STALLONE:
"That title, *Visual Commentary on the Come-from-Nowhere Pugilist Who Makes Good*, still sounds pretty damned rocky to me."

TED BUNDY to PATRICK HENRY:
"Give me liberty or give me death."

TED BUNDY to W. SOMERSET MAUGHAM:
"Sometimes, I feel as if I'm invincible. Other times, I feel as if I'm walking the razor's edge."

ELLSWORTH BUNKER to AMBROSE HILL:
"I'll bet if the two of us ever got together it would be bloody hell."

BUGS BUNNY to DR. SAM SHEPPARD
"What's up, Doc?"

PAUL BUNYAN to ROY CRANE:
"I said, 'Of course, it's going to make that noise. It's a buzz saw you're using.'"

PAUL BUNYAN to FELIX E. FEIST, JOE ANSON, NICK GRINDE, FRANK BUTLER, FRED FINKELHOFFE, and ELAINE RYAN:
"Oh, Babe's gotten around all right. Just off the top of my head, I can recall her in Baghdad, in Toyland, and on Broadway."

PAUL BUNYAN to LILLIAN HELLMAN:
"Yes, you're right. We did have a bit of a problem with that when we first teamed up. Our solution, of course, was a simple one. Babe merely started shitting in another part of the forest."

PAUL BUNYAN to WILLIAM P. MC GIVERN:
"Heat? You don't know what big is until you've seen Babe in hers."

PAUL BUNYAN to MELVILLE SHAVELSON:
"So, I finally told the complaining Mr. Hamilton — 'George, I'm a big man. Therefore, I cannot help but cast a giant shadow. If that interferes with your sunning, do us both a big favor, quit bitching, and move down the beach.'"

PAUL BUNYAN to STYX:
"And this is my blue-ox Babe."

WARREN EARL BURGER to SINCLAIR LEWIS:
"Don't talk to me about Barbara Walters! Did I tell you about the time 'Bab' bit me?"

DELTA BURKE to ANNE BOLEYN:
"I hear we're both getting the ax."

FRANCES HODGSON BURNETT to EDNA ST. VINCENT MILLAY:
"Never have I seen such a neglected, overgrown, secret garden. It took a whole day to separate a few figs from thistles."

GEORGE BURNS to SONNY JAMES:
"Cigars and good whiskey keep me young. Love knocked off a few years as well."

RICHARD BURTON to JOHN SEBASTIAN:
"I remember, as soon as Elizabeth and I had taken our marriage vows that second time, I turned to her, she turned to me, and we both blurted out, 'Welcome back!'"

GEORGE BUSH to THE BEACH BOYS:
"Barbara and I want to welcome you to the White House."

GEORGE BUSH to THE LOVIN' SPOONFUL:
"To bomb Iraq or not to bomb Iraq? Weighty decision. Did you ever have to make up your mind?"

GEORGE BUSH to RANDY TRAVIS, KATHY YOUNG and THE INNOCENTS:
"I was just going to say 'a thousand stars', but 'a thousand points of light' somehow seemed a thousand times better."

C

JULIUS CAESAR to ERIC BURDON and WAR:
"We purposely spill the wine, only a bit, as an offering to the gods."

JULIUS CAESAR to ADOLF HITLER:
"I came, I saw, I conquered."

JULIUS CAESAR to JOHN MONTAGU:
"That's right, a salad! Try and one-up me on that — if you think you can."

JULIUS CAESAR to STEVEN SPIELBERG:
"Et tu, Steven?"

CALIGULA to BLOOD, SWEAT and TEARS:
"And when I die, they'll naturally make me a god, but I didn't want to wait, so I became one in mortal form. So did my sister. Godliness runs in my family."

CALLINICUS OF HELIOPOLIS to JERRY LEE LEWIS:
"So, I said to Xaviera Hollander, 'If you really want to see great balls o fire, take a look at these.'"

CALLINICUS OF HELIOPOLIS to SAVONAROLA:
"So, you want the secret of getting all fired up?"

JAMES CAMERON to PAUL REISER:
"I know exactly what's eating you."

JOSEPH CAMPBELL to ABE BURROWS and JOHN STEINBECK:
"I knew the potential of condensed soups the minute my nephew, Dr. John Thompson Dorrance, showed me what he'd invented. I ran through cannery row, yelling, 'Can, can, as fast as you can!'"

MICHAEL CANE to BILL WITHERS:
"Lean on me."

MICHAEL CANE to HERMAN WOUK:
"The script was ludicrous after all the rewrites. The director was an alcoholic and an incompetent. They teamed me with a group of inept amateurs who couldn't act their way out of a paper bag. Not a professional, I'd venture to guess, among the whole bloody lot! I finally had enough, said, "Fuck you all!' and jumped ship."

AL CAPONE to MASSOUD BARZANI:
"So, you want to be a big cheese?!"

AL CAPONE to THIERRY HERMES:
"I don't care how you do it, but I want my money by Friday; so, you'd better scarf it up."

AL CAPONE to FRANK KING:
"I remember, during the war, gasoline was so scarce, we used to bootleg it in this one alley."

TRUMAN CAPOTE to DANTE ALGIHIERA:
"As soon as the play was over, I went backstage and said right out. 'Mr. Neil Simon, your comedy was simply divine.'"

TRUMAN CAPOTE to ENNIO DE CONCINI and PRIMO ZEGLIO:
"So, I said, 'Come on, Attila, hon; surely, we can work out something.'"

TRUMAN CAPOTE to C.S. FORESTER:
"Would you like me to tell you how Captain Horatio Hornblower, RN, got his name?"

TRUMAN CAPOTE to ARETHA FRANKLIN:
"Hell, Aretha! You call that a daisy chain? I call it a chain of fools."

TRUMAN CAPOTE to HUBERT GREGG:
"I don't know what Oscar Wilde did after the ball. I got up and went home."

TRUMAN CAPOTE to HALL AND OATES:
"Well, naturally, there's 'Kiss' on my list of all-time favorite rock groups."

TRUMAN CAPOTE to MICHAEL JACKSON:
"Rock Hudson? Sure, I knew him. Told him many times — 'Rock, with you, façade is too important. Who really gives a damn that you're as queer as a two-dollar bill?'"

TRUMAN CAPOTE to IRA LEVIN, GEORGE ABBOT, VAL GUEST, REGINALD BECKWITH, RICK NATKIN, SIDNEY J. JURIE, MART CROWLEY, WILL HAY, and ROBERT EDMUNDS:
"I've seen them all in my time. The boys from Brazil, from Syracuse, in blue, in brown, in Company C, in the band. All of whom proved that boys will be boys."

TRUMAN CAPOTE to MAUREEN MC GOVERN:
"Nine times out of ten, the morning after is a disaster."

TRUMAN CAPOTE to BILL MURRAY:
"What about Bob?"

TRUMAN CAPOTE to QUEEN:
"What's that crazy little thing called, Love?"

TRUMAN CAPOTE to DIANA ROSS:
"I swear, just before Rock Hudson got the part in *Giant,* he told me, 'I'm tired of the charade, and I'm coming out.' Of course, then he got the movie part, and it wouldn't have done at all for the public to think a pansy was playing opposite sexy Liz Taylor."

TRUMAN CAPOTE to RUBY and THE ROMANTICS:
"I told Oscar Wilde, 'Don't you worry, Oscar. Our day will come.'"

TRUMAN CAPOTE to SIDNEY SALKOW:
"Woe's be it for me to blow the dear man's cover. Suffice it to say — wasn't I surprised to discover the admiral was *a lady*?"

TRUMAN CAPOTE to JACK SHODER:
"Can you imagine the Truman-is-after-everything-in-pants nerve of that homophobe Norman Mailer? Of course, I played the complete innocent and asked, 'Why wouldn't you ever want to be alone in the dark with me Normie Pooh?'"

TRUMAN CAPOTE to FRANK SINATRA:
"I always found thrills and chills to making it with strangers in the night."

TRUMAN CAPOTE to REDD STEWART and PEE WEE KING:
"So, I walked right up to Mr. Williams at the ball, while the band played *Blue Danube,* and, brazen as you please, I asked, 'Tennessee? Waltz?'"

TRUMAN CAPOTE to THE ASSOCIATION:
"Well, I told her — 'You may be good at what you do, but never my love, baby!'"

TRUMAN CAPOTE to THE BROWNSVILLE STATION:
"Oh, sure, there was smokin' in the boys' room. But some of the other goings-on in there would have curled your hair."

TRUMAN CAPOTE to GENE TOWNE and GRAHAM BAKER:
"Someone once promised to show me *Broadway Joe* thru a keyhole. Just my luck, he only got it half right."

TRUMAN CAPOTE to PETER WEIR:
"Yes, well ... I do know all the scuttlebutt about him and Helen of Troy. But let me tell you a revealing little something about the cars that ate Paris."

TRUMAN CAPOTE to VICTOR WEST and BUDD LESSER:
"Can either or both of you picture me as a bandit?"

CAPTAIN AHAB to T.E.B. CLARKE AND HERMAN MELVILLE:
"I had William Maltese on board at the time. The white whale surfaced off our port bow. I pointed and said, 'Would you look at that barnacle, Bill, on Moby Dick?!'"

CAPTAIN NEMO to WINSOR MC CAY:
"You know, Winsor, I always regret not hearing the patter of at least one little Nemo around the place."

JUDY CARNE to JIM THORNBURG:
"Sock it to me, baby!"

KIM CARNES to HENRY BLANKE, WILLIAM WYLER, HENRY FONDA, and GEORGE BRENT:
"Okay, everyone say 'Nay' who doesn't want Bette Davis. Ayes have it. Do we agree?"

LESLIE CARON to SIDONIE COLETTE:
"Gee! Gee! How very nice for you to write something just for me."

BLAKE CARRINGTON to JOHN MC KESSON:
"You don't have to try and sell me on my own wife."

KRYSTAL CARRINGTON to NEIL DIAMOND:
"You're a real gem."

LEWIS CARROL to DIANA ROSS and THE SUPREMES:
"My original intention was for Narcissus to go through one of several looking glasses, but he was so hung up on just standing there, admiring his reflections, that I could never figure out how to get him started on through. Alice was a more willing subject."

JOHNNY CARSON to PERRY COMO:
"So, Orson Welles and Raymond Burr were presenting the Oscar. I couldn't help myself. I introduced the pair as *Round and Round*."

JOHNNY CARSON to ELMORE LEONARD:
"What do you get when Dolly Parton removes her bra?"

JOHNNY CARSON to ROD STEWART:
"People keep telling me, 'Tonight's the night,' or 'Gonna be alright,' but the first time, I admit to being as nervous as hell."

JOHNNY CARSON to GEORGE WORTHING YATES:
"You know what you'd have if Jim Henson and his group ever got mad and came after you?"

KIT CARSON TO JOYCE KILMER:
"I think that I shall never see a poem as lovely as a fur."

JIMMY CARTER to RAY CHARLES:
"I do confess. All the time I was in the White House, I had my peanut fields and Georgia on my mind."

JIMMY CARTER to VICKI LAWRENCE:
"Of course, I remember the night my brother Billy pissed on that power transformer. It was the night the lights went out in Georgia."

JIMMY CARTER to CHARLES SCHULZ:
"Damn right, there's money in peanuts."

GEORGE WASHINGTON CARVER to GEORGE WASHINGTON:
"Either of us could grow up to be president."

CASANOVA to AIR SUPPLY:
"Would I? Could I? Every woman in the world? Well ... maybe everyone but Roseanne (Barr) Arnold."

CASANOVA to LAJOS BIRD, ARTHUR WIMPERIS, and MAJORIE DEANS:
"Take it from me, 'Catherine the Great' wasn't."

CASANOVA to JAMES BRIDGES and EDWARD CHILDS CARPENTER:
"So, finally, after all these years, I've become the baby-maker. Or, how about the bachelor-father?"

CASANOVA to COCO CHANEL:
"Yes. Well, on a scale of one to ten, I'd only give you a five."

CASANOVA to CHICAGO:
"Once sex becomes a habit, it's a hard habit to break. Take it from me."

CASANOVA to PETULA CLARK:
"Damned right, I know a place. Just the place. Your place, or mine!?"

CASANOVA to NATALIE COLE:
"However, did you guess that I've got love on my mind?"

CASANOVA to CYRKLE:
"I got these colored prophylactics from Denmark, and I was wearing this bright red one and having sex with — actually, I can't remember with whom. What I do remember is that *whoever* wrapped her arms tightly around my neck, lifted her face up against mine, and whispered, 'You, love, are giving me one helluva red-rubber ball.'"

CASANOVA to DOROTHY FIELDS:
"I'm in the mood for love."

CASANOVA to GLENN FRY:
"Talk about hot! And she tells me that's probably because the heat is on. Talk about cold!"

CASANOVA to JAMES HEINZ:
"Variety is the spice of life."

CASANOVA to AMEDEO MODIGLIANI:
"My secret is nothing more nor less than long necking."

CASANOVA to ROBERT E. SHERWOOD:
"The age for love? Well, the first thing I ask myself is, 'Are they walking and talking?'"

CASANOVA to THE SYLVERS:
"You want a hot line? How about, 'Let's fuck!'?"

CASANOVA to THREE DOG NIGHT:
"Aphrodisiacs? I don't touch them. Swear to God. I've always found it easy to be hard."

CASANOVA to GINO VANNELLI:
"Sometimes I just wanna stop all this rutting before old age stops me. Most of the time, though, I'm content with the status quo."

JOHNNY CASH to RICHARD OUTCALT:
"I told that clothing salesperson, 'Buster, brown is not what I want. Is that too hard for you to understand?'"

FIDEL CASTRO to ROBERT REDFORD:
"Sorry, Bobby. You may be in Havana, but there's no cigar this time!"

CHATTY CATHY to JOE JONES:
"I know you're not going to believe this. Who could? I mean, the notion is so absurd. Nonetheless, he said it. No two ways about it. Plain as the nose on your face. Big as life. Walked right up to me, brazen as you please. Didn't even wait for an introduction. Oh, no, not him. God knows where he was when his parents were telling him about the rudiments of good manners, because he has none now. I mean…."

CEO OF MACK DIESEL TRUCKS to CASANOVA:
"No one says not even you can't be a really good trucker if you just set your mind to it."

CEO OF MATTEL TOYS to EDWARD KENNEDY:
"And Marketing agrees we've got a winner in Teddy Bare."

ERNST BORIS CHAIN to SAM COOKE:
"Yes, I do confess. All through high school, I had this compulsion to form a gang of my very own."

MARGE AND GOWER CHAMPION to QUEEN:
"Let us tell you who we are, and you just try making something of it."

NORA CHARLES to FRANCES GOODRICH:
"Oh, I was after 'the Thin Man' for years before I finally landed him."

CHEVY CHASE to SAMMY JOHNS:
"'Chevy,' Van Johnson said, 'I'd like to be in your next film.'"

CHUBBY CHECKER to CHARLES DICKENS:
"I always figured Oliver Wendell Holmes a bit straitlaced. Until the night of the party when everyone started chanting, 'Twist, Oliver, twist!' And, he got up and really showed us how it was done."

MAURICE CHEVALIAR to SIDONITE COLETTE:
"Ah, chérie, how good it is to see you again."

JULIA CHILD to BILL BIXBY, SUSAN CLARK, DAVID WAYNE:
"Okay. Today's lesson is how to make the apple dumpling, gang."

JULIA CHILD to BOOKER T. AND THE MGs:
"I do believe the Jolly Green Giant had green bunions and green onions, considering what he does for a living."

JULIA CHILD to BREAD:
"I kneaded you. You needed me."

JULIA CHILD to SITTING BULL:
"The secret of mastering custard is all in the beating."

JULIA CHILD to GEORGE GORDON (LORD) BYRON:
"So, she came up and said, 'Julia Child, Harold Wilson; he's a real fan of yours.' And wasn't I pleased as punch!?"

JULIA CHILD to TRUMAN CAPOTE:
"The press got it all wrong. What I said was fruit *compote*."

JULIA CHILD to FRANK CARNEY:
"I mean, this guy is pharaoh of Egypt, right? You'd think he'd serve one helluva meal. But, no! It was so bad, I finally had to go right up and say, 'Don't you have a pizza, Tut?'"

JULIA CHILD to GEORGE ELIOT:
"Pepper mill and dental floss are the two things I'm never without."

JULIA CHILD to NICK GILDER:
"Picture this. New York City. August. Temperatures in the hundreds. No air-conditioning. Me over a hot stove. A culinary creation with main ingredient of red chili peppers. I don't have to tell you to what all of that added up, do I?"

JULIA CHILD to BREWSTER HIGLEY:
"When I cook on your range, I really feel at home."

JULIA CHILD to K.C. and THE SUNSHINE BAND, and FLEEETWOOD MAC:
"Luckily, my husband likes to eat, which complements my penchant for cooking. During the course of some of my more adventuresome elaborate meals, he often encourages me with a, 'Keep it comin', Love. Don't stop now.'"

JULIA CHILD to BARRY MANILOW:
"Yes, a cake. Looks like we made it together. However, my advice to you is not to give up your day job."

JULIA CHILD to WOLF MANKOWITZ:
"You look like a man who enjoys a delicious dessert with almonds and raisins. Have a taste of this."

JULIA CHILD to ROBERT MARASCO:
"I'm afraid all today's inept class has to show for itself is burnt offerings."

JULIA CHILD to DEAN MARTIN:
"Now, pay attention, because memories are made of this."

JULIA CHILD to BOBBY PICKETT and THE CRYPT KICKERS:
"Well, I have seen large fried potatoes, and I have seen big boiled potatoes. But never have I seen such monster mash potatoes."

JULIA CHILD to TERENCE RATTIGAN:
"There is one school of thought that says a roast should be prepared merely by sticking it in a pot and adding a bit of water. Today, though, I'm going to show you the browning version."

JULIA CHILD to DEE DEE SHARP:
"You guessed it. It's mashed-potato time!"

JULIA CHILD to DONNA SUMMER:
"Careful! That stove top is covered with hot stuff."

JULIA CHILD to THE NEW EDITION:
"Yes, I see you've got it boiling nicely, but it's time to cool it now."

JULIA CHILD to H.M. WALKER:
"Yes, I see. It's another fine mess, isn't it? My advice, 'Don't give up your writing job, no matter how much you'd prefer being a cook.'"

THOMAS CHIPPENDALE to WILLIAM KEMMLER:
"Give that man the chair."

AGATHA CHRISTIE to EUGENE O'NEILL:
"Do you believe Kitty Kelley! She wrote that I had an illegitimate daughter, Anna. What's more, I've heard she's sold the movie rights."

JULIE CHRISTIE to THE CONTOURS:
"When did I break it up with Warren Beatty? I guess it was the day I finally asked him, 'Do you love me?'"

MADONNA LOUISE CICCONE to ALEX HALEY:
"The worst thing about blonde-out-of-a-bottle is that constantly I have to keep searching for my black roots."

ERIC CLAPTON to SALLY FIELD:
"Go ahead, lay down, Sally. I promise I'll like you in the morning."

T.E.B. CLARKE to ERIC HUGHES:
"Against all odds, Michael Pertwee and I wrote *Against the Wind*."

CLAUDIUS to FYODOR DOSTOYEVSKI:
"Don't play the idiot with me!"

CLAUDIUS to THE ORIONS:
"Mah-marvelous specimen. Bra-brought from Africa. Cah-called, I believe, a Wah-Watusi."

WARD CLEAVER to OSCAR HAMMERSTEIN:
"June had breast augmentation and is virtually busting out all over."

CLEOPATRA to JOHANNES GUTENBERG:
"Sorry, you're just not my type."

DOCTOR CLITTERHOUSE to BARRE LYNDON, MURIEL ROY BOLTON, LIONEL JEFFRIES, BERT I. GORDON, MARK HANNA, and RICHARD CHAPMAN:
"Think I'm amazing, do you? I suggest you check out Dr. X, Mr. Blunden, The Colossal Man, and some Dobermans of my acquaintance."

GLENN CLOSE to MICHAEL DOUGLAS:
"I can't stop loving you."

WILLIAM FREDERICK CODY to CHARLES W. POST:
"I used to tell them that if they had letters, post 'em; I'd do my best to get them delivered."

KEVIN COE to JACK FINNEY:
"I always wanted to make an assault on a Queen. Elizabeth II, maybe, or Truman Capote."

RUTH COE to DAEDALUS:
"Watch out for son!"

SEBASTIAN COE to THE VENTURES:
"All the time, my mother kept telling me, 'Walk, don't run,' but it wasn't walking I wanted to do."

COLLEAGUES OF WILLIAM RAMSAY to WILLIAM RAMSAY:
"Why don't you find a way to lighten up?"

PHIL COLLINS to JOAN and PETER FOLDES:
"I remember when I was with *Genesis,* Walt Disney had this idea of doing animated bits about the band as a regular Saturday-morning kiddy show. We said, 'Thanks, Walt, but no thanks.'"

PHIL COLLINS to THE FIXX:
"You know how one thing leads to another on the dance floor, against all odds, even in these days of AIDS? I told *Men Without Hats* that someone should come up with a dance named for a prophylactic in order to get the safe-sex message across."

CHRISTOPHER COLUMBUS to PEARL BUCK:
"I'll tell you one thing that isn't two. After being at sea all those days, nothing can get any better than the feel of the good earth under your feet."

JOSEPH CONRAD to JIM BAKKER:
"You'd better ask forgiveness of the Lord, Jim, or you're sure to end up in hell for all the wrongs you've done."

WILLIAM CONRAD to JAY AND THE AMERICANS:
"The cameraman kept telling Orson Welles and me to come a little bit closer together. Finally, I had to come right out and say that I was sorry, but we were already as close as was physically possible, until one or both of us lost a few pounds."

CALVIN COOLIDGE to MIKHAIL LERMONTOV:
"Charles Lindbergh; now, there was a hero of our time."

DAVID COPPERFIELD to BACHMAN-TURNER OVERDRIVE:
"You like that trick? Well, you ain't seen nothing yet."

HOWARD COSSEL to JOHN O'HARA:
"I'll always remember that game, John — Butterfield: 8; North Frederick: 10."

KEVIN COSTNER to KEVIN COSTNER:
"I know just what this picture needs, but...."

KEVIN COSTNER to THE DRIFTERS:
"We were at this party — myself, Virginia Woolf, Thomas Wolfe. I went up and told both to save the last dance for me."

MARY CRANE to ARTHUR MARX, ROBERT FISHER, and ROBERT BLOCH:
"No doubt about it. I should have called the Bates Motel to cancel my reservation. But how was I to know I'd end up with some psycho in the shower?"

WES CRAVEN to CURTIS MAYFIELD:
"So, I got to thinking. What if there was this child molester, name of Freddy, see. He's killed by irate parents, see. But he comes back to life — sort of — like in every kid's nightmares. You know, a Freddy's dead but not dead sort of thing."

MONTE CRISTO to ALEXANDER DUMAS:
"One, two, three, four, five, six, seven..."

DAVY CROCKETT to JOHN DENVER:
"I've seen my share of big cities and city folk. Frankly, I always thank God I'm a country boy."

LORAINE CROOK to AARON MONTGOMERY WARD:
"Always remember the one about *the check's in the mail*."

CHRISTOPHER CROSS to BOB SEGER AND THE SILVER BULLET BAND:
"God, I love sailing against the wind."

TOM CRUISE to ANDREW HUBBLE BEARDSLEY:
"It was horrible. I've never before had such a bad case of gas. Nights and days of *thunder*."

ROBINSON CRUSOE to SAMMY CAHN:
"I don't need to tell you it's been a long, long time."

ROBINSON CRUSOE to BRENDA LEE:
"Every morning on that island, before Friday, I'd wake up and say to myself, 'All alone am I.' It was a horrible feeling, let me tell you."

ROBINSON CRUSOE to BOBBY VINTON:
"Talk about one very Mr. Lonely."

PIERRE CURIE to MARIE CURIE:
"My dear, you look positively radiant tonight."

GEORGE ARMSTRONG CUSTER to ELVIS PRESLEY:
"So, I sent a message back to Sitting Bull. 'Surrender? You have to be kidding!'"

D

LEONARDO DA VINCI to HENRY JAMES:
"Come over here. I want you to meet Mona Lisa and see my portrait of the lady."

DAEDALUS to BILL CONTI:
"Oh, I should have known Icarus was overconfident, just by the way he flapped those wax wings and said, 'Gonna fly now!' The young fool!"

DALLAS COWBOYS CHEERLEADERS to THOR HEYERDAHL:
"Rah, rah, rah!"

ROGER DALTREY to JOHNNY RIVERS:
"Of course, Peter Townshend could be as rowdy as the rest of us. But to judge him exclusively by that is to see only the poor side of Town."

HERSCHEL DANIELOVITCH to SCOTT JOPLIN:
"Hey, man! You on the rag, or what?"

CLARENCE DARROW to JIM PALMER:
"Can I see your briefs, Mr. Palmer?"

CHARLES DARWIN to MUHAMMAD ALI:
"I suppose butterflies do dance, and bees certainly do sting."

CHARLES DARWIN to JOHN SCOPES:
"Right. Man from monkeys. Horseflies from Pegasus."

CHARLES DARWIN to DICK TRACY:
"A yellow jacket does get attention."

DAVID (THE ISRAELITE) to THE STEVEN MILLER BAND:
"When I was facing Goliath of Gath on that battlefield, I knew it was all up to one little rock 'n' me."

BENNY DAVIS to GEORGE NELSON:
"You know, you've got a baby face."

BETTE DAVIS to EDWARD KENNEDY:
"All you think about is peter, peter, peter."

BETTE DAVIS to A.A. MILNE:
"What a dump!"

SAMMY DAVIS, JR. to SAM AND DAVE:
"Hell, yes, I've got soul, man!"

SAMMY DAVIS, JR. to THE HAPPENINGS:
"It's true what those white folks say. I got rhythm!"

SAMMY DAVIS, JR. to JOHN GREENLEAF WHITTIER:
"I knew I was cocaine-bound from my very first sniff."

DORIS DAY to THE HOLLYWOOD ARGYLES:
"Dogs need plenty of exercise, and I walk mine here everyday. The only problem is that every dog-lover in the neighborhood uses this same alley — Oop!"

HONORE DE BALZAC to THE BEATLES:
"So, don't you know, in walks George Sand, and I say to Chopin, 'Who is that man?' Naturally, Chopin laughs and informs me, 'That's no man; she's a woman.'"

VENUS DE MILO to ERNEST HEMINGWAY:
"Actually, somewhere in my life I was forced to give a farewell to arms."

VENUS DE MILO to RONALD REAGAN:
"Arms? Arms? I don't know anything about arms."

MADAM DE POMPADOUR to RAY CHARLES:
"You don't know me, but to know me is to love me."

MADAM DE POMPADOUR to GEOGE MICHAEL:
"Be sure to wake me up before you go-go, so I can show you the way to the throne room."

MADAM DE POMPADOUR to RUBY AND THE ROMANTICS:
"Warren Beatty says to me, 'So, you've got this thing going with Louis XV. You see it as an obstacle. I don't. In fact, I can tell you with time-proven confidence, our day will come.'"

MARQUIS DE SADE to MICHAEL JACKSON:
"Beat it!"

MARQUIS DE SADE to THE MARCELS:
"Give me Kevin Costner for one evening, and I can promise him a blue moon for his next movie."

MARQUIS DE SADE to W. SOMERSET MAUGHAM:
"Have I got tales to tell of human bondage?!"

MARQUIS DE SADE to THE DAZZ BAND:
"Frankenstein brought his monster, and then, as usual, couldn't control it. I finally said, 'If it wants to whip, let it whip.' As if any of us could have stopped it."

MARQUIS DE SADE to THE DOVELLS:
"I promise to love you until you can't sit down."

MARQUIS DE SADE to TIMMY THOMAS:
"I know that Leopold von Sacher-Masoch wants to ask me, 'Why can't we live together?'"

VITTORIO DE SICA to THE BEATLES:
"Here's your choices: yesterday, today, and tomorrow."

TOMAS DE TORQUEMADA to ADOLPHUS W. GREEN:
"Let's check the stakes for today's burnings. Hmmmm. Now, this one is almost an A-1 stake. Saws, though, should be used to trim off both ends. Wouldn't you agree?"

JAMES DEAN to EDDIE RABBIT:
"Every time I get in that car of mine, I feel as if it's drivin' my life away."

MARJORIE DEANS to BARBARA PAYTON:
"Knowing who you married, I'll bet you'll agree, 'Aren't men beasts?'"

JOHN DENVER to LABELLE:
"I'm sorry, lady. Marmalade is what I ordered. Not jelly. Not jam. Marmalade. Preferably orange."

JOHN DENVER to VALENTIN YOSHOV, GRIGORI CHUKRAI, JOHN CRAWFORD, EDWARD PENNEY, BO WIDERBERG, HAROLD SWANTON, and SHOHEI IMAMURA:
"Sure, guys, I've a whole repertoire of ballads. Of a soldier. Of Cable Hogue. Of Joe Hill. Of Josie. Of Narayama. Which'll it be?"

DEVIL to PETER FRAMPTON:
"Time to get an exorcist, Peter, 'cause I'm in you."

FRANCESCO DI PIETRO DI BERNARDON to BUDDY DE SYLVA and LEW BROWN:
"The best things in life are free."

JOHN THOMAS DIAMOND to LORELEI LEE:
"Tell them about your best friend."

CHARLES DICKENS to STYX:
"It was the best of times. It was the worst of times."

DION to RUBY KEELER:
"I saw you in *Gold Diggers of 1933*, Ruby, baby, and you were fantastic!"

DIRTY HARRY to WILLIAM C. PROCTOR:
"You'd better come clean!"

DIRTY HARRY to NANCY and FRANK SINATRA:
"Go ahead. Do somethin' stupid and make my day!"

WALT DISNEY to CLAUS VON BULOW:
"And, I'm thinking, *Sleeping Beauty,* where the heroine is put into a coma by…"

JEANE DIXON to ROGER MILLER:
"I could have predicted something like this. The way James Dean drove that car of his, you could tell he thought himself king of the road."

JEANE DIXON to ISAAC NEWTON:
"I see a cookie."

JEANE DIXON to ROBERT STARR:
"What sign are you?"

DOCTOR DOLITTLE to NEIL TENNANT and CHRIS LOWE:
"Better to face the fact that you're never going to make it in music. Come work in my pet shop, boys, where you'll at least be assured three square meals a day and a roof over your heads."

DOCTOR JOHN THOMPSON DORRANCE to HAMMOND INNES:
"No doubt but that my invention of soup condensation provided my uncle, Joseph Campbell, with his own little kingdom."

DOCTOR JEKYLL to WOLFGANG PUCK:
"I'll be eating alone. So, a table for two, please."

DOCTOR SPOCK to MARY MARTIN:
"Nothing to worry about, Mary. You've just reached a stage."

DON JUAN to ALEXANDER POPE:
"Casanova is such a sex maniac, you could put him in a locked room and he'd try to rape the lock."

DON JUAN to THE SUPREMES:
"I guess I can sum up my successes by saying I've always followed that tried-and-true maxim that you can't hurry love — unless there's a disgruntled husband banging on the door."

PHIL DONAHUE to PAUL MC CARTNEY and KENNY ROGERS:
"Coming up on our show, Dr. Hook advocates 'Don't Fall in Love with a Dreamer,' and Kim Carnes shows the ladies how to apply mascara and makeup for sexy eyes."

SAM DONALDSON to DASHIELL HAMMET:
"As a boy, I always had my mother telling me, 'Sam, spade the garden. Sam, spade the garden.' All of which turned me off to ever becoming a farmer."

GEORGE DONNER to AL JOLSON and BUDDY DE SYLVA:
"California, here I come — I hope."

DONOVAN to OLIVIA NEWTON-JOHN:
"Have you never been mellow yellow?"

HILDA DOOLITTLE to HUGH LOFTING:
"Mother always wanted me to marry a doctor."

KIRK DOUGLAS to HORATIO ALGER:
"Since my father literally sold rags for a living, and I haven't done all that badly, it's kind of a rags-to-riches story, wouldn't you say?"

MIKE DOUGLAS to YVONNE ELLIMAN:
"So, Glenn Close says to me, 'If I can't have you, no one can!' Talk about downright blood-chilling."

DRACULA to ABBOT and COSTELLO:
"I'd like you to meet Frankenstein, the Invisible Man, the Mummy, the killer Boris Karloff, Dr. Jekyll and Mr. Hyde."

DRACULA to ALICIA BRIDGES:
"No doubt about it. I love the night life."

DRACULA to ALFRED BRYAN:
"So, I said to Miss Peggy Lee, 'I am flattered. But as far as you becoming the Peg o' my heart, forget it!'"

DRACULA to PHIL COLLINS and THE COMMODORES:
"Do you know what it's like being forever on the nightshift, one more night after one more night, stretching into centuries?"

DRACULA to ALEC COPPEL and JEAN COCTEAU:
"Oh, I suppose, if you insist. I do remember, there was one particularly black night when I was especially hungry for the blood of a poet."

DRACULA to ENGLAND DAN and JOHN FORD COLEY:
"I'd really love to see you tonight."

DRACULA to MELVIN FRANK, JACK ROSE, and CHARLES B. GRIFFITH:
"I'm an advocate of Emily Post good manners, and do my very best to exhibit a touch of class while eating, even though some of my peers, as often as not, make due with a bucket of blood."

DRACULA to HERMAN'S HERMITS:
"Naw. I'll prove it to you. Come over here. That's right. Put your ear against my chest. Now, can't you hear my heartbeat?"

DRACULA to LAUREL AND HARDY and JOHN MICHAEL HAYES:
"You want busy bodies, check out any graveyard after dark. But not for me, because there isn't a blood-filled specimen among them."

DRACULA to MANFRED MANN'S EARTH BAND:
"Quite frankly, it's an eye condition. Every time I go out into the sun, I'm literally blinded by the light."

DRACULA to RAFAEL SABATINI:
"Well, I'm picky, but not that picky. I mean, given the choice of admiral blood or captain blood, I wouldn't necessarily suck the former first, every time."

DRACULA to STARBUCK:
"Even before all these present down-on-the-sun revelations, by the medical profession, as regards aging and skin cancer, I knew, intuitively, that moonlight feels right."

DRACULA to THE CLASSICS IV:
"Yes, I saw the movie *Ghost.* Frankly, I prefer something more spooky."

DRACULA to THE ZOMBIES:
"So, I go to the coffin for Vampira, and guess what? She's not there."

DUKE KAHANAMOKU to JUDGE ROY BEAN:
"Let's hang ten."

DUKE KAHANAMOKU to THE BEACH BOYS:
"I've surfed South Africa, Australia, South America, even Great Britain. Take my word for it, surfin' U.S.A. is the best surfin' of all."

ISADORA DUNCAN to A.J. LERNER and F. LOEWE:
"I could have danced all night."

JIMMY DURANTE to THE SYLVERS:
"I tell you, if anyone knows the nose, I do. And there is, indeed, a complication referred to in medical texts as *Boogie Fever*."

E

AMELIA EARHART to LENORE COFFEE:
"Who else but Warren Beatty?! I told him — 'Maybe, Warren, if it were another time, another place. But now, on the wing of a plane, at twenty-thousand feet? I think I'll pass this time.'"

AMELIA EARHART to LEO ROBIN:
"Do you know, sometimes I wish I could just disappear beyond the blue horizon."

GEORGE EASTMAN to PAUL SIMON:
"The way my lawyers see it, your *Kodachrome* is a blatant patent infringement."

SHEENA EASTON to ANTOINE DE SAINT-EXUPERY:
"They can say all they want about Prince Rogers Nelson, but he'll always be the *little* Prince to me."

CLINT EASTWOOD to HUGO MONTENEGRO, HIS ORCHESTRA AND CHORUS:
"I'd like you all to meet Mother Teresa, Al Capone, and the Phantom of the Opera."

THOMAS ALVA EDISON to CLAUDINE CLARK:
"And I call my invention *Party Lights*."

THOMAS ALVA EDISON to EDDY GRANT:
"It's my goal to make electric avenue-lights all over America."

DAVE EDMUNDS to THE TEMPTATIONS and TONY ORLANDO AND DAWN:
"I hear you knocking. Was it just my imagination running away with me, or did you knock three times?"

EDWARD VIII to LANGSTON HUGHES:
"When I abdicated for the woman I love, I knew it was a one-way ticket."

KARL ADOLF EICHMANN to CHER:
"What most people fail to realize is that gypsies, tramps, and thieves, not just Jews, were included within *the Final Solution*."

ALBERT EINSTEIN to MAJOR-GENERAL BENEDICT ARNOLD:
"You've simply got to try and get the point."

DWIGHT D. EISENHOWER to IRVING BERLIN:
"Blue skies — that's what we desperately need for D-Day."

DWIGHT D. EISENHOWER to JEANNE D'ARC:
"I know what's at stake here. Do you?"

ELSIE THE BORDEN COW to HERMAN MELVILLE:
"No wonder the term *shoot the bull!* All he did, all day long, was stay on his side of the fence and go, 'Moo, moo, moo.' Finally, I just walked up and said, 'Oh, moo to you, too!'"

ELSIE, THE BORDEN COW to LOUIS PASTEUR:
"I suppose you'll milk this for all it's worth."

ERNESTINE to MUAMMAR QADAFI, SADDAM HUSSEIN...:
"One ding-a-ling, two ding-a-ling…"

EVE to HAROLD MELVIN AND THE BLUE NOTES:
"Talk about slow-mover! I finally had to tell him — 'Adam, if you don't know me by now, it's not likely you ever will.'"

EVE to HELEN REDDY:
"You want stupid? I had to tell him — 'I'm not supposed to have one, Adam. I am woman.'"

J.R. EWING to OSCAR MAYER:
"Let's hope you can bring home the bacon as well as your Daddy did."

EXCITORS to ANNETTE BENING:
"You want to have Warren Beatty's baby. Well, you might tell him that, but we don't know what good it will do, if any, do we?"

EXILE to XAVIERA HOLLANDER:
"How much to kiss you all over, and vice versa?"

FAGIN to JOHN GAY:
"The way I figure it, that opera of yours is going to have to go begging."

FARMER BROWN to DAVID H. LAWRENCE:
"It was my argument that a man couldn't have enough sons. But wouldn't you know, Casanova jumped right in with, 'And lovers.'"

FATHER OF MEL GIBSON to MEL GIBSON'S MOTHER: "What shall we name him, honey?"

FAUST to THE BEE GEES:
"I guess what cinched the deal was Old Jack telling me, 'I promise you, two weeks in heaven is too much heaven. Booorring!'"

RICHARD FEVEREL to GEORGE MEREDITH:
"Never, but never, have I experienced such an ordeal."

MARSHALL FIELD to FERDINAND MAGELLAN:
"I'm talking a major sale here."

HENRY FIELDING to ALAN LE MAY:
"I was desperate for a name. Then, along came this singer at whom all the ladies threw their undergarments. Right then and there, I knew my search was over."

HAMILTON FISH to BOBBY FREEMAN:
"The water is great. C'mon and swim."

CARRIE FISHER to THEODORE DREISER:
"I never guessed, but *The Righteous Brothers* told me, 'We always wanted a sister, Carrie.'"

EDDIE FISHER to THE BEATLES:
"Finally, I had to break down and tell Mike Todd — 'Truth is, she loves you. That doesn't mean I've stopped loving Liz.'"

EDDIE FISHER to ANDY WILLIAMS:
"I couldn't help it. When Liz ran off with Mike Todd, I called her on the phone and told her, 'I can't get used to losing you.' She told me, 'Now, you know how Debbie felt.'"

EDDIE FISHER to CAREY WILSON:
"On the one hand, there was Debbie Reynolds, to whom I was married. On the other hand, there was Liz Taylor, to whom I had all intentions to marry."

F. SCOTT FITZGERALD to GORDON LIGHTFOOT:
"So, you want to do a song about the wreck I've made of my life, do you? Well, let me tell you one thing that isn't two. You had better not use my real name, or I'll sue you all of the way from here to Tuesday."

RHONDA FLEMING to THE BEACH BOYS:
"John Payne was aptly named. All during the filming of *The Eagle and the Hawk*, he was always 'Help me, Rhonda,' with this, or "Rhonda, help me' with that. Apparently, no one ever bothered to tell him that the good Lord helps those who help themselves."

FLOWER THE SKUNK to THE J. GEILS BAND:
"Love stinks!"

KEN FOLLETT to MELANIE:
No doubt you've heard of *Key Largo*, *Key to the City*, and *The Keys to the Kingdom*. Well, I've got a brand new key."

DAME MARGOT FONTEYN to JULIAN MITCHELL, STANLEY PRICE, and PIERRE MARTON:
"None of you will ever be another Rudolf Nureyev if you don't master the arabesque."

ANDREW HULL FOOTE to THE SANGRI-LAS:
"Remember, walkin' in the sand is good for your arches."

HARRISON FORD to THE ROLLING STONES:
"Sad but true, there are some mornings I wake up, feeling like my namesake, and wishing there was someone special to start me up."

HENRY FORD to JOSEPH CAMPBELL:
"What do you think? It's got eight, not six cylinders. So, there's all that additional juice. I'm calling it V-8."

HENRY FORD to JOHN MASEFIELD:
"Take it from me. Any Japanese car goes kaput far faster than the more solid American-made."

JOHN THOMSON FORD to MARY TODD LINCOLN:
"Aside from that, Mrs. Lincoln, what did you think of the play?"

NATHAN BEDFORD FORREST to ROBERT SHERWOOD:
"To be candid, I was absolutely petrified at the time."

JOHN FORSYTHE to JOHN GALSWORTHY:
"I thought I'd take all of my stories from my days on the *Dynasty* set and call it THE FORSYTHE SAGA. In the end, my publisher recommended I drop the title as too pompous."

BOB FOSSE to CAROLE KING:
"Don't give me all that jazz, man!"

STEPHEN FOSTER to BARRY MANILOW:
"I write the songs. What do you do?"

JEAN-BERNARD-LEON FOUCAULT to EDGAR ALLAN POE:
"It's just up your alley. I figure you could call it, *The Pit and the Foucault*."

FOUR-AND-TWENTY BLACKBIRDS to HENRY FORD:
"Caw! Caw!"

FOUR TOPS to BERNADETTE PETERS:
"Bernadette!"

MICHAEL J. FOX to ETIENNE MONTGOLFIER:
"Can you give me a lift?"

FRANKENSTEIN (DOCTOR) to BROOKLYN BRIDGE:
"So, I said to Dracula, 'What's the worst that can happen?'"

FRANKENSTEIN (DOCTOR) to BOBBY DARIN:
"So, he looks at me with those pathetic, blood-shot eyes, and he says, with genuine feeling, 'You're the reason I'm living.'"

FRANKENSTEIN (DOCTOR) to GORDON DAWSON and SAM PECKINPAH:
"Nothing was going right. Then, I had a big breakthrough after having told Igor to bring me the head of Alfredo Garcia."

FRANKENSTEIN (DOCTOR) to MADONNA:
"Get me the right material, girl, and I can make you a lover who'll be crazy for you."

FRANKENSTEIN (DOCTOR) to LEO SAYER:
"Oh, I know Igor has this reputation as some kind of perfect servant. But let me tell you, there have been many times I've had to take him aside and tell him, 'If you're not here when I need you, you're liable to find yourself out on the street without a pot to piss in.'"

FRANKENSTEIN (DOCTOR) to NEIL SEDAKA:
"Putting together isn't all that difficult, once I have the body parts. On the other hand, breaking up is hard to do."

FRANKENSTEIN (DOCTOR) to THE CLIMAX BLUES BAND:
"You know, I had my suspicions from the start. Oh, it walked, and it talked, but I just knew I couldn't get it right."

BENJAMIN FRANKLIN to FRANCIS SCOTT KEY:
"Oh, say, can you see?"

SIGMUND FREUD to THE ANTICHRIST:
"It was quite a revelation to learn everyone's ills can be attributed to sex, sex, sex."

SIGMUND FREUD to JOHANN BACH:
"It's perfectly okay to play with your organ."

SIGMUND FREUD to IRVING BERLIN:
"There Lucifer was, in my office, and he says to me, 'You want to know what I dream? I dream of a white Christmas.'"

SIGMUND FREUD to BERTRAND BLIER:
"Whenever I'm in a Scandinavian country, someone invariably asks, 'Buffet, Freud?' and leads me off to this very long table heaped high with food."

SIGMUND FREUD to SKEETER DAVIS:
"So, I said to Warren Beatty — 'No, Warren, I don't really think it will be the end of the world when you can't get it up any more.'"

SIGMUND FREUD to FLEETWOOD MAC:
"No doubt about it. The secrets of men's psyches lie in their dreams."

SIGMUND FREUD to ROBERT FULTON:
"You want to live to a ripe old age, you'd better learn to let off steam."

SIGMUND FREUD to GUS KAHN:
"I'll see you in my dreams."

SIGMUND FREUD to BRENDA LEE:
"So, after six years of analysis, I finally got Al Capone to confess, 'I want to be wanted.'"

SIGMUND FREUD TO RANDY NEWMAN:
"I diagnose your case as classic midgetphobia."

SIGMUND FREUD to ARNOLD PALMER:
"It's important to learn how to get teed off."

SIGMUND FREUD to JOAN RIVERS:
"Can we talk?"

SIGMUND FREUD to DAMON RUNYON:
"You want a classic no-no? I'm talking guys and dolls. You want a happier life, leave the dolls to the little girls."

SIGMUND FREUD to THE MONKEES:
"It has been my experience that the worst kind of dreamer is the daydreamer believer."

BENJAMIN FRANKLIN to THE VILLAGE STOMPERS:
"Thomas Jefferson? A-OK. John Adams? So-so. George Washington? Square, from the word go."

SIGMUND FREUD to SAMUEL B. WEST and HARRY RELIS:
"Silly name for a sailing captain — Sinbad. Silly for anyone, really, in its redundancy."

SIGMUND FREUD to STEVIE WONDER:
"So, I said to Don — 'Damn-it, you're so uptight, I can see where you got the name Knotts.'"

BETTY FRIEDAN to JESUS CHRIST:
"I suppose you think your God's gift to women?!"

G

PETER GABRIEL to ALAN O'DAY:
"Just between you and me, I'm here on earth as an undercover angel."

ERNEST GALLO to ERVIN DRAKE:
"For our burgundy, it was a very good year."

JULIO GALLO to ADOLPH COORS:
"Whining won't get *you* anywhere."

MOHANDAS KARAMCHAND GANDHI to E.M. FORSTER:
"I was in South Africa at the time, but after much soul-searching, I booked a passage to India and entered politics to protest British sedition laws."

MOHANDAS KARAMCHAND GANDHI to JEAN GIRAUDOUX:
"India is a land of constant surprises. I remember, one morning, I got up to find a tiger at the gate."

ALEXANDER GARDEN (DOCTOR) to LOUIS ANTOINE BOUGAINVILLE:
"Give yourself a little time, and you, too, will blossom."

AVA GARDNER to NEIL SIMON, JOSEPH L. MC EVEETY, JAMES GUNN, FRANCIS SWANN, NICO KATSIOTES, and JOSEPH L. MANKIEWICZ:
"Look, guys, I'm not the only one who enjoys going barefoot in the park. Just today, I've seen an executive, a mailman, and one whole army battalion. Not to mention the Contessa over there."

GARGANTUA to THE DIAMONDS:
"I've seen *small* in my time, but, no doubt about it, Dr. Ruth Westheimer is really a little darlin'."

RICHARD J. GATLING to DANNY GLOVER:
"You want to talk a lethal weapon?"

RICHARD J. GATLING to THE ROLLING STONES:
"See this gun? If I pull its trigger, it'll be damned hard to miss you. My advice to you, therefore, is to cut the caterwaulin' and do so right now."

MAESTRO GEPPETTO to WILLY SHOEMAKER:
"Your whole future rides on whether or not you decide to make shoes."

RICHARD GERE to THE CAPRIS:
"She really likes Kevin Costner. So, when I asked her to go with me to see *Dances with Wolves*, and she hesitated, you know what I said to cinch the deal? 'There's a moon out tonight.'"

FRANK GIFFORD to PETER HYAMS and KURT VONNEGUT:
"So, at half time, the score was Capricorn, one, and Slaughterhouse, five."

KING C. GILLETTE to BOOTH TARKINGTON:
"There's nothing mightier than the pen — rod and sword included."

ALLEN GINSBERG to BLONDIE:
"The tide is high, and so am I. The stars are out, and so will I be — pretty soon. Want a toke?"

ALLEN GINSBERG to JOHN F. WALLACE:
"Can you dig it, man?"

ALLEN GINSBERG to WALT WHITMAN:
"Might I suggest you change the title to something less controversial than *Leaves of Marijuana*?"

CARTER GLASS to BLONDIE:
"Hell, yes, I'm concerned. Wouldn't you be if you heard Dr. Frankenstein had told Igor to get your heart?"

JOHN HERSCHEL GLENN to CORNELIUS BROTHERS AND SISTER ROSE:
"When I felt the rockets ignite, I said to myself, 'It's too late to turn back now.'"

HELENA GLINSKI to SIR WALTER SCOTT:
"All day long I'd beg him, 'Ivan, hoe the garden!' But he was a terrible boy, even lazier than that kid, Sam Donaldson, and he grew up to be an even more terrible man."

GOLDILOCKS to MICHAEL RITCHIE:
"So, I said — 'Here's the bad news, Bears. I've made a mess of things. The good news? I don't plan on sticking around that much longer.'"

GOLIATH to EDNA FERBER:
"Three guesses what I am."

GOLIATH to ELVIS PRESLEY:
"So, Miss Betty Friedan says to me, 'A big hunk o' love doesn't count for anything in my book.'"

RAUL GONZALES to WAYNE NEWTON:
"Well, my daughter doesn't take too many walks with me these days. She's really tired, I guess, of always having to say, 'Daddy, don't you walk so fast.'"

JANE GOODALL to TARZAN:
"Someone's tried to make a monkey out of you."

PATRICIA GOZZI to BLONDIE:
"I'm really excited about it. There's this mentally unstable girl, see. She has a tragic romance with a fugitive murderer. It's going to be directed by John Guillermin. And I'm getting to act with Dean Stockwell and Melvyn Douglas."

SHEILAH GRAHAM to DUANE EDDY:
"Loretta and Gig gave the studio a hard time, and their publicists insisted they only did it, 'Because they're Young.'"

SHEILAH GRAHAM to TOMMY ROE:
"All my friends call me *Sheilah*. You can call me *Miss Graham*."

ULYSSES SIMPSON GRANT to CALVIN KLINE:
"Dress right, dress!"

MERV GRIFFIN to JAMES BEARD:
"You're certainly not *my* Beard; so, what is it with the press that they keep asking what I've got cooking?"

GRIM REAPER to JOHN DONNE:
"Me? Proud? Hell, no!"

JOSEPH GUILLOTIN (MADAM.) to JOSEPH GUILLOTIN (MONSEUR.):
"If we're to pay these bills, you simply have to find a way to get ahead."

GUINEVERE to ELVIS PRESLEY:
"Oh, Merlin warned me, all right. 'One knight to avoid,' he said, 'is Lancelot!'"

GUNNAR AND MATTHEW NELSON to FOREIGNER:
"No, you needn't see a doctor for double vision."

ARSENIO HALL to ALBERT EINSTEIN:
"Pat Sajak? He, as an emcee, is square."

HAMLET to BEN-GAY:
"Aye, there's the rub!"

OSCAR HAMMERSTEIN to SALLY FIELD:
"I like you. I really like you."

ANDY HARDY to ROSE ROYCE:
"So, I said — 'Hey, gang! I know how we can make some money. How about a car wash?'"

DEBORAH ANN HARRY to CHIC YOUNG:
"So, I heard this *Blondes Have More Fun* hair-coloring campaign, right? And I gave it a try. After which, we called ourselves *Blondie*. As for more fun, well…"

GARY HART to BRUCE SPRINGSTEEN:
"As far as I can remember, Xaviera Hollander has said a total of maybe two words to me — ever. 'Hungry, Hart?' And that, please note, was at a dinner party."

FRANCIS BRETT HARTE to GENE PITNEY:
"Sure my family and I have some rough times. But take it from me — only love can break a Harte."

GOLDIE HAWN to FREDA PAYNE:
"It's true. Goldfinger, Missy Gold, Golda Meir, Bobby Goldsboro, an I, are going to form a band and call it — can you guess what?"

NATHANIEL HAWTHORNE to PROPSER MERIMEE:
"I fought long and hard to call it CARMINE A, but my publisher insisted that title just *wouldn't fly*."

WILLIAM RANDOLPH HEARST to EUGENE JOSEPH MC CARTHY:
"You make me see red!"

HUGH HEFNER to ELVIS PRESLEY:
"I remember at the wedding, saying to myself, 'Hef, no doubt about it; it's now or never.'"

ERNEST HEMINGWAY to IRVING BRECHER:
"Look, it's simple. You line the pheasant up in the gun sights. That's this. You pull the trigger. That's this. And it's bye-bye birdie."

ERNEST HEMINGWAY to HUNTINGTON HARTFORD:
My advice to you, 'Bag it.'"

ERNEST HEMINGWAY to ELBERT HUBBARD:
"I wanted an interview with Frederico, but I couldn't seem to get it. Finally, I told his secretary. 'Take this message to Garcia Lorca. He sees me now, or I'm back to the States on the next plane.'"

ERNEST HEMINGWAY to VICTOR HUGO:
"I've been in many a Paris whorehouse, my friend. Take it from me, on the whole, their lays? Miserable!"

ERNEST HEMINGWAY to HENRIK IBSEN:
"My advice? When in the wild, duck, or you'll end up with bird shit on your head or bear shit on your boot."

ERNEST HEMINGWAY to TOMMY JAMES:
"The old man's problem was that he didn't exert enough effort to drag in the line. Had he done so, he wouldn't have lost the damned fish to the shark."

ERNEST HEMINGWAY to ALAN JAY LERNER:
"Oh, I don't know how to explain it. There was, though, a different *feel* to being an American in Paris just after the war."

ERNEST HEMINGWAY to HAROLD ROBBINS:
"I remember John Huston and I wanted new carpets, so we went on safari and bagged fifteen zebras, each, to make them."

ERNEST HEMINGWAY to LAURENCE STERNE:
"You want a generous drink for your money? Not one better than Tristram's shandy at the Ol' Ale House in London."

TIPPI HENDREN to B.J. THOMAS:
"I remember saying to Hitchcock, that very first day of shooting, 'Alfred, raindrops keep falling on my head.' He put his arms around me, gave me a reassuring hug, and said, 'I'm afraid those aren't raindrops, my dear.'"

DON HENLEY to MEN AT WORK:
"I was just down under the bleachers, and you won't believe the dirty laundry hanging over my head."

HENRY VIII to BAD COMPANY:
"Food and women will be my downfall. I can't get enough of either."

HENRY VIII to HERMIT'S HERMITS:
"I'm Henry VIII, I am. Who are you?"

HENRY VIII to SHIRLEY JACKSON:
"We have always lived in a castle."

HENRY VIII to MICKEY ROONEY:
"Once is not enough."

HENRY VIII to THE YOUNG RASCALS:
"Well, I might have married a seventh time, but I had been disappointed so often, I kept asking myself of every woman who came along, 'How can I be sure of this one?'"

MATTHEW A. HENSON to LECH WALESA:
"Yes, I'll be glad to take you all of the way to the north with me, Pole."

KATHARINE HEPBURN to ? (QUESTION MARK) AND THE MYSTERIANS:
"Oh, yes, *The African Queen*, and all that location shooting. I remember the on-water shots, of course, but the bush was especially hazardous. Brambles, don't you know. One evening alone, I counted ninety-six tears in one skirt."

HERCULES to THE ESSEX:
"Cleaning out those stables was easier said than done."

PEE WEE HERMAN to A TASTE OF HONEY:
"Oh, look! A boogie! Oogie! Oogie!"

PEE WEE HERMAN to K.C. AND THE SUNSHINE BAND:
"I stuck my finger in my nose, pulled out a big one, and said to Mr. Lew Landers, 'I hear you're looking for a Boogie Man. Well, I'm it.'"

PEE WEE HERMAN to ROY ORBISON:
"You think it's only the lonely who frequent adult-movie theaters? Hell, no!"

PEE WEE HERMAN to THE DOORS:
"Touch me."

PEE WEE HERMAN to STEVIE WONDER:
"Anyone with even a modicum of smarts could tell the hankie she'd used before coming out on stage hadn't done the job. So, this jerk keeps leaning over to me and asking why everyone is whispering. I finally pointed out the obvious, 'Boogie on reggae woman.'"

THIERRY HERMES to NANCY SINATRA:
"I'm afraid none of these boots are made for walkin', rather for ridin'. Are you sure you can't persuade Frank to buy you a horse?"

JAMES HERRIOT to THEODORE ROETHKE:
"So, I say, 'Where is this sick cow of yours?' And he points to this tiny speck, barely visible on the horizon. 'In the far field,' says he. 'Better get walking if you hope to get there before nightfall.'"

MILTON SNAVELY HERSHEY to SAMMY DAVID, JR.:
"If anyone can, I can."

MILTON SNAVELY HERSHEY to JACKIE GLEASON:
"How sweet it is!"

THOR HEYERDAHL to MAXWELL ANDERSON:
"Like everyone else, drinking can make me high."

CATALYTIC QUOTES

HIAWATHA to JAMES FENIMORE COOPER:
"You want to see pollution? They've been dumping toxic-waste drums along the Mohawk for years."

HIAWATHA to HENRY WADSORTH LONGFELLOW:
"I'll be calling you … oooo … oooo … oooo … oooo … oooo … oooooo."

JAMES BUTLER HICKOK to STEPPENWOLF:
"No doubt about it. I was born to be wild."

BENNY HILL to JAMES FORD BELL:
"Cheerio, old boy! Cheerio! Cheerio!"

BENNY HILL to GOGI GRANT:
"Let's not call it *flatulence* but *wayward wind*."

EDMUND HILLARY to ROBERT BURNS:
"You may see my body here in the valley. But, take it from me, my heart's in the highlands."

EDMUND HILLARY to DIANA ROSS:
"I used to just say, 'Ain't no mountain high enough.' Then, I proved it when I stood atop Everest."

HIROHITO to KYU SAKAMOTO:
"I do confess to loving a large plate, now and again, of sukiyaki."

HIROHITO to THE ANIMALS:
"You may call it my castle, but we Japanese call it the house of the rising sun."

HIROHITO to THE BEATLES:
"Yes, you're quite right. On 19 March 1924, one of our submarines, No. 43, was in a collision off Sasebo."

ALFRED HITCHCOCK to EDDIE RABBIT:
"Admittedly, it was a step by step process, but when I had it in the can, I knew I had myself a marvelous, four-star, comedy thriller."

ADOLF HITLER to JAMES L. KRAFT:
"'Vel, Veeta,' I said to her. 'Vhich vay does the vhippervill go?'"

ADOLF HITLER to THE BEATLES:
"Yes, I did once get Meyer Rothschild's attention by screaming, 'Hey Jude!'"

ADOLF HITLER to USA FOR AFRICA:
"*You*? Don't make me laugh! Germany. *We* are the world!"

HO CHI MINH to PEACHES AND HERB:
"I don't care what anyone says, my one and only aim was to see north and south Vietnam reunited."

LAURA Z. HOBSON to CHARLES F. RICHTER:
"Let's shake on it."

DUSTIN HOFFMAN to EDDIE RABBIT:
"When I was asked to do it, I naively thought — 'Why not? I love a rainy night as well as the next guy.'"

DUSTIN HOFFMAN to THE FOUR SEASONS:
"In *Tootsie*, when I was *in drag*, one of my major problems in making the character come off as real was that I had this hard-broken tendency to walk like a man."

PAUL HOGAN to ROLF HARRIS:
"Tie me kangaroo down, sport."

PAUL HOGAN to TERRY JACKS and GORDON LIGHTFOOT:
"Actually, I prefer my seasons in the sun down under."

PAUL HOGAN to ELTON JOHN:
"Bloody hell if it isn't a crocodile! Rock, mate! Get a rock!"

PAUL HOGAN to MATTEL TOYS:
"Mates, there's nothing hotter than a good Barbie."

HAL HOLBROOK to LAMAR TROTTI and HENRY JAGLOM:
"When I first met my wife, my reaction was 'Can this be Dixie Carter?' My second was, 'Can she bake a cherry pie?'"

XAVIERA HOLLANDER to BLONDIE:
"You have definite potential. Call me."

XAVIERA HOLLANDER to BLONDIE and IRVING BERLIN:
"Just call me madam."

XAVIERA HOLLANDER to CHER:
"A lot of people think my life has been nothing but one bang bang after another."

XAVIERA HOLLANDER to RACHEL CROTHERS:
"As husbands come and as husbands go, my cash registers keep ringing accompaniment."

XAVIERA HOLLANDER to JEFFREY DELL:
"I finally told him, 'Don't take it to heart, it's hard to be good.'"

XAVIERA HOLLANDER to DURAN DURAN:
"Well, look who's here! If it isn't the wild boys."

XAVIERA HOLLANDER to GEORGE GERSHWIN:
"So I said to Michelangelo Buonarroti, 'You mean, not only did you do that wonderful stuff while on your back, but you got paid for it, too. Nice work if you can get it.'"

XAVIERA HOLLANDER to FRANK D. GILROY, RUSSEL ROUSE, and TONY O'GRADY:
"Was the man in question the fastest gun alive? No. He arrived at the stroke of nine. Some guys, you just touch and *Bang*!"

XAVIERA HOLLANDER to LEWIS GREIFER and DAVID T. CHANTLER:
"Come on, gentlemen. Give me a break. When hasn't mine been a cash-on-demand business?"

XAVIERA HOLLANDER to MANOS HADJIDAKIS and JULIUS J. EPSTEIN:
"Never on a Sunday, guys. But come around any Wednesday."

XAVIERA HOLANDER to HALL AND OATES:
"You want a maneater, she's extra."

XAVIERA HOLLANDER to MARK HARRIS:
"Henry Drummond a clergyman? And to think the catch-phrase around here was always, *Bang the Drum slowly.*'"

XAVIERA HOLLANDER to ELTON JOHN:
"I had more than one of my girls tell me that her perfect night would be *a bennie* and the Jets."

XAVIERA HOLLANDER to LARRY L. KING and PETER MASTERSON:
"Had the deal gone through, J.R. Ewing my silent backer, I would have had the best little whorehouse in Texas."

XAVIERA HOLLANDER to ROBERT FRANKLIN LESLIE:
"The Chicago Bears and I? If anything did happen, you can bet I'm saving it for my book."

XAVIER HOLLANDER to HENRY WADSWORTH LONGFELLOW:
"Whyever didn't you call first? I must look like the wreck of the Hesperus."

XAVIERA HOLLANDER to JERRY MATHERS:
"My, you are an eager beaver."

XAVIERA HOLLANDER to JOE MC CARTHY:
"'Franz Mesmer,' I said, 'no doubt about it — you made me love you.'"

XAVIERA HOLLADNER to JOHNNY MERCER:
"So, I said to Mr. Mathis: 'Johnny, you do, indeed, have that old black magic.'"

XAVIERA HOLLANDER to NICK (THE GREEK):
"I suppose you want a piece of the action."

XAVIERA HOLLANDER to FREDERICK BURR OPPER:
"Was Patrick Hooligan ever happy? I'd say, he was bound to have been, at some time in his life, wouldn't you?"

XAVIERA HOLLANDER to NEIL PATERSON and CHARLES WILLIAMS:
"Talk about innocent sinners. I finally had to come right out and say — 'Come on, guys, it's your money. Don't just stand there.'"

XAVIERA HOLLANDER to LLOYD PRICE:
"So, I said to Mr. Quasimodo — 'I'm really afraid there's nothing we can do for you.' And, he says, 'Hell, lady, I've got personality. Doesn't that count for something?'"

XAVIERA HOLLANDER to PETE ROSE:
"Boy, do you have balls."

XAVIERA HOLLANDER to DIANA ROSS:
"I always told my girls to be up front with every customer and tell him right out, 'If you want to touch me in the morning, it'll be extra.'"

XAVIERA HOLLANDER to PAUL SCHRAEDER:
"I never handled male prostitutes. Something about the notion of an American gigolo didn't fit the package I was selling. Maybe if I'd set up business in France, or Italy, it might have been different."

XAVIERA HOLLANDER to ZELDA SEARS and EVE GREEN:
"Look, you're at the wrong place. It's Elizabeth Arden who has beauty for sale."

XAVIERA HOLLANDER to THE SHIRELLES:
"Oh, sure, momma said a lot of things. Did I pay attention? — that's another question."

XAVIERA HOLLANDER to JIMMY SOUL:
"If you wanna be happy, baby, let Xaviera make you happy."

XAVIERA HOLLANDER to THE BEATTLES:
"Please you? Please you? How about please, please me for a change?"

XAVIERA HOLLANDER to THE FOUR LADS:
"You boys are truly in for some moments to remember."

XAVIERA HOLLADNER to THE TEMPTATIONS:
"You call this an orgy? I call it a ball of confusion."

XAVIERA HOLLANDER to THE THREE DEGREES:
"Thanks, and when will I see you again?"

XAVIERA HOLLANDER to THREE DOG NIGHT:
"I often wonder if my choice of profession had anything to do with the fact that mama told me not to come."

XAVIERA HOLLANDER to MIKE TODD:
"Yes, I've heard of round the world, but in eighty days is a new one."

XAVIERA HOLLANDER to TOMMY JAMES AND THE SHANDELLS:
"How did I know they were underage? Honey, I didn't have to have genius I.Q. They told me they'd come for a little *hanky-panky*, if you can believe."

XAVIERA HOLLANDER to DAN TOTEROH:
"Honey, what we have here is just about all that money can buy."

XAVIERA HOLLANDER to BILL WALSH and DON DAGRADI:
"And here's our box of available accoutrements. As you can see, we have handcuffs, whips, chains, ropes, masks, hoods, dog collars, leashes, bed knobs and broomsticks."

XAVIER HOLLANDER to ARTHUR WEISS and ART ARTHUR:
"Would you believe I hadn't even thought of around the world *under the sea* until I met Jacques Cousteau?"

XAVIER HOLLANDER to WILLIAM K. WELLS and PERRY VERKROFF:
"Well, for certain, Paul Bunyan was one memorably big boy."

XAVIERA HOLLANDER to NEIL YOUNG:
"I don't care what they say, I'm one hooker who didn't have a heart of gold."

JOHN HENRY HOLLIDAY (DOC) to SINCLAIR LEWIS:
"I said, 'We're going to have to pull out the arrow, Smith; even then, there's sure to be complications.'"

JOHN HOLMES to SIDNEY BUCHMAN, JACK TOWNLEY and JEROME CHODOROV:
"Actually, the producers had to look all over town to find anyone to take all of me."

JOHN HOLMES to WILLIAM DE VAUGHN:
"Be thankful for what you've got. Do you know how many women have turned me down just because of what I have?"

JOHN HOLMES to DAN FOGELBERG:
"Ya-hooooo! Didn't I tell you mine was longer?!"

JOHN HOLMES to SAMUEL FULLER:
"I do remember one shoot where everything kept going wrong. Before it was over, everyone was calling my you-know-what *the big red one*."

JOHN HOLMES to PHILIP MACKIE:
"In my business, you're out on your ass the very moment you can no longer get you-know-what all the way up."

JOHN HOLMES to ELVIS PRESLEY:
"You think you're too much!? Man, check me out in the shower room."

JOHN HOLMES to LOU RAWLS:
"You can look high and low, even in this business known for pulling well-endowed gents out of the woodwork, but you'll never find another *love* like mine."

JOHN HOLMES to DIANA ROSS:
"It just looks endless, Love."

JOHN HOLMES to AL WILSON:
"Okay, Al, it's your turn to show and tell."

SHERLOCK HOLMES to KIRK DOUGLAS:
"I'm investigating a gunfight at the O.K. Corral."

SHERLOCK HOLMES TO GEORGE EASTMAN:
"Picture this. He calls me in and says, 'Mr. Holmes, skip all this deductive-reasoning bullshit and just show me that my wife has been sleeping around.'"

SHERLOCK HOLMES to GUS KAHN:
"By pure deduction, Mr. Kahn, it had to be you."

SHERLOCK HOLMES to LITTLE PEGGY MARCH:
"This is how it will work. You will pay me. I will follow him and will get back to you as soon as I can."

SHERLOCK HOLMES to GENE RAFFERTY:
"Yes, I live on Baker Street."

SHERLOCK HOLMES to THE CLASSICS IV:
"Traces of arsenic and old lace should have made those murders easy enough to solve."

SHERLOCK HOLMES to GENE WILDER:
"You think I'm smart and led a fast life?! You should meet my brother and hear his adventure."

RAYMOND HOOD to e. e. cummings:
"I mean, talk about an enormous room, have you seen Radio City Music Hall?"

ROBIN HOOD to ERIC CLAPTON:
"I shot the sheriff with my trusty bow and arrow."

ROBIN HOOD to WALTER FERRIS and JOSEPH HOFFMAN:
"I always figured the only good Sheriff of Nottingham was a Sheriff of Nottingham at sword's point."

CAPTAIN HOOK to MAC DAVIS:
"I finally had to tell her, 'Baby, don't get hooked on me.'"

BOB HOPE to PETER, PAUL, AND MARY:
"Know what you've got when you've got Herb Alpert in Hurricane Lisa?"

BOB HOPE to PROCOL HARUM:
"Every morning, when I was in makeup, in would come our director, Norman Z. McLeod, and scream at the makeup person, 'No! No! I want him a whiter shade of pale!'"

BOB HOPE to PHILIP YORDAN, JACK ROSE, and MEL SHAVELSON:
"My intention was to visit our men in war and always leave them laughing."

JACK HORNER to COLONEL HARLAND SANDERS:
"Talk about finger-lickin' good."

HARRY HOUDINI to EDMUND HALLEY:
"First you see it, then you don't."

MOE HOWARD to THE CHIFFONS:
"Larry? He's so fine, as a comedian, that my brother and I did far better with him than without him."

ROCK HUDSON to GEORGE MICHAEL:
"I worry about someone making that one careless whisper that will shoot my he-man image all to hell."

ROCK HUDSON to THE BOOGEYMAN:
"You say, 'Come out of your closet.' I say, 'You first!'"

HOWARD HUGHES to HILDA DOOLITTLE:
"This place is really a steal at one-million-five. Six bedrooms. Eight baths. Pool. View of the sea. Garden."

HUMBERT HUMBERT to GABRIELE D'ANNUNZIO:
"Yes, I did come to look upon Lolita as the child of pleasure come into my life."

HUMBERT HUMBERT to STEVE LAWRENCE:
"Do you know how many times I saw Lolita and tried to tell her, 'Go away, little girl'?"

HUMBERT HUMBERT to RINGO STARR:
"So, I said to Lolita — 'Sure, you're sixteen. And, I'm one of The Beatles.'"

ENGELBERT HUMPERDINCK to HENRY FIELDING:
"That's right. Singer name of Tom Jones. Women actually throw their underwear on the stage whenever he performs."

ENGELBERT HUMPERDINCK to JAKOB GRIMM:
"I said to this little girl, 'Don't you find *Hansel and Gretel* a somewhat grim fairy tale?'"

MERCY HUMPPE to HERMAN RAUCHER and ANTHONY NEWLY:
"You tell me. Can Hieronymous Merkin ever forget me and find true happiness?"

HUMPTY DUMPTY to FRANK TUTTLE:
"What we need here is compromise. So, I'll tell you and Frederick Stephani about all the king's horses. I'll tell Robert Rossen about all the king's men."

SADDAM HUSSEIN to NAPOLEON XIV:
"They think they're going to take me away, ha-haa. But I'm out the door long ahead of them."

ANGELICA HUSTON to RAY CHARLES:
"All I have to say about Jack Nicolson at this time is that, yes, I did tell him to hit the road."

I

HENRIK IBSEN to BRUCE JOEL RUBIN:
"I wanted to expand upon what you did."

IGOR to SHEENA EASTON:
"You should be flattered that Dr. Frankenstein passed over Bette Davis to put in a special order for your eyes only."

IGOR to THEODORE GERICAULT:
"So, it's three o'clock in the morning, right? Dr. Frankenstein wakes me up and says, 'Get dressed. I need you to go out and get me two legs and an arm.'"

IGOR to EDWARD MADDEN:
"I always dug up the best parts when I did it by the light of the silvery moon."

JACK to THE SUPREMES:
"I mean, a really nasty fall. So, I say to Jill — 'I know you're all right. Come see about me.'"

JACKSON FIVE to DAVID PURSALL and JACK SEDDON:
"ABC, you're dead! DEF, you're dead! GHI, you're dead!"

MICHAEL JACKSON to PAUL MC CARTNEY:
"I know I said the girl is mine, but I changed my mind. You can have her."

JAYNETTS to SALLY FIELD:
"You're table is number fifteen. Sally, go 'round the Roses at table ten, since Pete is not in the best of moods since his suspension."

THOMAS JEFFERSON to DOCTOR FRANKENSTEIN:
"All men are created equal."

JOCASTA to ANDY GIBB:
"Oedipus, more than once, told me, 'I just want to be your everything.' How much he ended up being just that is the real tragedy, isn't it?"

BILLY JOEL to PAUL MC CARTNEY, MICHAEL JACKSON, HALL AND OATES:
"So, I told Mel Tillis and Cyndi Lauper that before I married my uptown girl, it was my experience that girls just want to have fun. Cyndi agreed. All Mel could come up with was, 'Say-say-say it isn't so.'"

BILLY JOEL to THE SPANDAU BALLET and HALL AND OATES:
"I suppose I could say it isn't so, but it's true that my wife was an uptown-girl."

OSA JOHNSON to LOUISA MAY ALCOTT:
"And out of the jungle appeared these pygmies — little men and equally little women. Charming!"

OSA JOHNSON to THE DOOBIE BROTHERS, HARRY ESSEX, and ARTHUR ROSS:
"We found this lagoon with really black water. It looked like a potential breeding ground for all sorts of creature."

ROBERT JOHNSON to WALLACE STEVENS:
"How's about a little of my deep-blues-style guitar?"

JOLLY GREEN GIANT to THOMAS KENSETT:
"How many more times am I going to have to tell you to can it?!"

JOLLY GREEN GIANT to THE BROTHERS FOUR:
"Nothing makes me happier than seeing row upon row of green fields."

JOLLY GREEN GIANT to THE KINGSMEN:
"Give me one good reason why I shouldn't slap you with violate trade-mark?"

INDIANA JONES to JIM MORRISON:
"You had better spend more time out of doors, or your health is likely to suffer the consequences."

TOM JONES to KITTY KELLEY:
"What's new, pussycat?"

JANIS JOPLIN to THE BEE GEES:
"For me and Bobby McGee, there were some long and lonely days."

JAMES JOYCE to ULYSSES SIMPSON GRANT:
"I know I promised you a biography, but I just can't seem to get enthused by the Civil War. How about if I come at it from an entirely different angle?"

K.C. AND THE SUNSHINE BAND to CARLY SIMON:
"Keep it comin', love, because nobody does it better."

DIANE KEATON to DUSTY SPRINGFIELD:
"Warren Beatty? Isn't that old news?! Well, what can I say, but to point out that I knew what I was getting. From the outset, I told him, 'You don't have to say you love me.' Nor did he ever."

RUBY KEELER to LYMEN BAUM:
"What if I changed my last name to Slippers? Do you think that would make me more famous?"

RUBY KEELER to THE ROLLING STONES:
"It was a Friday. I remember it clearly. And the head of this major auction house calls me up and says, 'I kid you not, Ruby, Tuesday we're auctioning off a pair of your slippers.'"

KITTY KELLEY to BILLY JOEL:
"Do you believe it? That asshole wrote a book about my life? My life for Christ's sake!"

KITTY KELLEY to MARGARET LANDON:
"My next book? I'm seriously looking at this long-time relationship between Anna and the King of Siam."

EDDIE KENDRICKS to KOOL AND THE GANG:
"Jungle boogie down? What's that mean?"

EDWARD KENNEDY to BEETHOVEN:
"The party is BYOB, so don't forget your fifth."

EDWARD KENNEDY to ELVIS PRESLEY:
"So, I walked right up to her in the bar and said, 'Let me be your Teddy, bare.'"

JOAN KENNEDY to SUZI QUATRO and CHRIS NORMAN:
"I first realized I had a drinking problem when it dawned on me that I was doing a lot of stumblin' in and out of places. You know?"

JOAN KENNEDY to THE ROLLING STONES:
"After living with Teddy caused my nineteenth nervous breakdown, I finally decided I'd had enough."

JOHN F. KENNEDY to THE MAMAS AND THE PAPAS:
"What could I do when Jackie confronted me about my ongoing affair with Marilyn Monroe? I told her — 'You're right. I saw her again.' It would have done none of us any good to lie about it."

ROSE KENNEDY to BETTE MIDLER:
"Is it true you're starring in a movie about me?"

FRANCIS SCOTT KEY to BENJAMIN FRANKLIN:
"Go fly a kite!"

GEORGE K. KHUNOV to STEPHEN CRANE:
"Well, I like to think that I didn't do anything anyone else wouldn't have done. But, yes, I did get the *Red Badge of Courage*."

NICOLE KIDMAN to SMOKEY ROBINSON:
"No doubt but that I enjoyed Tom Cruise 'n *Days of Thunder*. I married him, didn't I?"

KING ARTHUR to GEORGE BENSON:
"Give me the knight who offended, and I'll personally see he's punished."

KING ARTHUR to MICHAEL HOGAN:
"Of course, I would have liked some Arabian knights, but there's the religious thing."

KING ARTHUR to THE EAGLES:
"Take a look. One of these knights is going to betray me."

KING ARTHUR to THE MOODY BLUES:
"Talk about a drag ball, I never saw so many knights in white satin."

KING MIDAS to IAN FLEMING:
 "Obnoxious little twerp, so I gave him the finger."

KING MIDAS to CLIFFORD ODETS:
 "All it took was one touch, and William Holden became my very own golden boy."

DON KING to LUTHOR:
 "For this fight, I've lined up Superman, but *Luthor versus Superman* isn't going to draw tiddly. How about we call you Atom Man?"

DON KING to JIMMIE RODGERS:
 "So, she said, 'You want to get anywhere with me, honey, comb your hair.'"

JEAN KING to JOHN HOLMES:
 "Hey, Mr. big Stuff!"

JOHN KING to BULLDOG DRUMMOND:
 "Are you palming an ace, Drummond? Or, does it just look as if you're cheating?"

MARTIN LUTHER KING, JR. to JOHN DONNER:
 "Some call it white on black, others call it black on white. I call it integrated copulation."

MARTIN LUTHER KING, JR. to JOSEPH HAZELWOOD:
 "Black is beautiful!"

MARTIN LUTHER KING, JR. to JOHN C. HIGGINS:
 "The black sleep, just as the white do. And when they get up, each puts his pants on, one leg at a time."

MARTIN LUTHER KING, JR. to THE ROLLING STONES:
 "In this country, if you want it spat upon, paint it black."

NEL KING to W.D. RICHTER:
 "All night long? Well, you're not the only one. I did, too. So did Peter Achilles. And what's a list like this without Warren Beatty and William Maltese?"

CATALYTIC QUOTES 75

BUDDY KNOX to DOLLY PARTON:
"Come on. What do you say to just you and I having a party, Doll?"

DAVID KOPAY to PERCY SLEDGE:
"Can you please tell me just what the big deal, when a man loves a woman?"

DAVID KOPAY to THE TROGGS:
"You take a look at John Holmes in the shower and tell me he doesn't have a wild thing."

EDWARD I. KOCH to J.W. BLAKE and C.B. LAWLOR:
"So, I said to the police chief, 'With the crime in this city the way it is, you wouldn't catch even me on the sidewalks of New York after dark.'"

RONALD KRAY to W. SOMERSET MAUGHAM:
"I'll bet you the moon and sixpence that my brother and I can make your publisher pay up."

FRIEDRICH KRUPP to SAMUEL COLT:
"You're going to have to stick to your guns."

LADY GODIVA to WILLIAM S. BURROUGHS:
"Let's do lunch."

LADY GODIVA to JOHNNY PRESTON:
"I tell you, it's well-known in Palm Beach that Teddy Kennedy has this penchant for running bare."

LADY GODIVA to LEVI STRAUSS:
"You're panting."

LADY MAC BETH to MR. CLEAN:
"Out damn spot!"

FERNANDO LAMAS to HENRIK IBSEN:
"You know Arlene, don't you? Well, I hadn't seen her in years. Then, one day, I was at Hedda Hopper's, and Hedda up and says, 'Let's go over to Dahl's house.'"

LOUIS L'AMOUR to THE BEATLES:
"It took years for publishers to take me seriously and look upon me as something more than just another pulp-paperback writer."

ANN LANDERS to DARRYL ZANUCK:
"A movie about me? Oh, I really think not, but thanks anyway."

JOHN LANDIS to SYLVESTER STALLONE:
"This is your one and only chance to get an Oscar."

LASSIE to ELTON JOHN:
"Have you seen who they signed as my co-star? To put it frankly, the bitch is back."

LINDA LAVIN to DAMON RUNYAN:
"People were always coming into *Mel's Diner* and ordering the blue-plate special."

LINDA LAVIN to WILLIAM SHAKESPEARE:
"The things that Mel would come up with. 'We'll combine ham and eggs,' he'd say, 'and call it a hamlet.' As if he'd never heard tell of a ham omelet."

STEVE LAWRENCE to PETULA CLARK:
"What did I do when I heard Donny Osmond singing *Go Away Little Girl*? I went right up to him and told him just what I though. Namely, 'This is my song, you little twit!'"

T.E. LAWRENCE to ANTOINE DE SAINT-EXUPERY:
"What do I miss about Arabia? The wind, the sand, the stars."

T.E. LAWRENCE to LORRAINE HANSBERRY:
"It's been my experience that here, in Arabia, there's not much, by way of farm produce, to be raisin' in the sun."

T.E. LAWRENCE to JACK HULBERT, GUY BOLTON, and W.P. LIPSCOMB:
"Shhhhh. The camels are coming."

T.E. LAWRENCE to NORMAN SCHWARZKOPF:
"Some desert storms are really quite short-lived."

MERVIN LE ROY to BRIAN HYLAND:
"I told those idiots at Warner Brothers that I wanted to direct a picture about a gypsy woman. What do they give me? A script about some stripper."

ROBIN LEACH to IVES W. MC GAFFNEY:
"Sucks? I'll tell you what sucks!"

LOUIS LEAKY to RANDY TRAVIS:
"Put succinctly, I suppose, yes, I do spend an inordinate amount of time digging up bones."

TIMOTHY LEARY to EDMUND HILLARY:
"Hey! Want to get high?"

TIMOTHY LEARY to CLARK KENT:
"And I tell *you*, LSD is the only way to fly."

HANNIBAL LECTER to THOMAS BAUM:
"Actually, I once stalked Art Carney, only because I'd come across this marvelous recipe for chili con."

HANNIBAL LECTER to NAPOLEON BONAPARTE:
"You look good enough to eat."

HANNIBAL LECTER to FOREIGNER:
"If you think you're hot-blooded now, wait until you've been in that pot awhile longer."

HANNIBAL LECTER to ALLEN GINSBERG:
"You're going to pot."

HANNIBAL LECTER to ROBERT HICHENS, DOROTHY FARNUM and JOHN COLTON:
"Dracula hears the call of the blood. Jack London hears the call of the wild. I, on the other hand, hear the call of the flesh. As happens, I hear yours calling, 'Eat me! Eat me!' right this moment."

HANNIBAL LECTER to PATRICK KIRWAN, BLANAID IRVINE, SCOTT DARLING, WILSON BROWN, GUY BOLTON, SONYA LEVIEN:
"Yes, once I did make broth of a boy of the streets. I forget the kid's name, but the soup was delicious."

HANNIBAL LECTER to CARLO LIZZANI, MONJA DANISCHEWSKY, TED WILLIS, and LESSER SAMUELS:
"People can be genuinely bitter. I remember that to be markedly true of Mr. Rice, Mr. Springs, Mr. Harvest and, ironically enough, Mr. Sweet."

HANNIBAL LECTER to RICHARD LLEWELLYN, RICHARD BLACKBURN, and PAUL BARTEL:
"I suppose you wouldn't believe me if I told you many of my meals, like eating Raoul, was catch as catch can?"

HANNIBAL LECTER to SANTA CLAUS:
"Definitely a pot belly!"

BRUCE LEE to CARL DOUGLAS:
"Guy's name is Michael Allen. He's written this movie with lots of kung-fu fighting. So, I tell him, 'Hey, Michael, go no farther in looking for a star. I'm your man!'"

ROBERT E. LEE to DOUGLAS WALLOP:
"Damn, Yankees!"

JACK LEMMON to THE BUCKINGHAMS:
"Frankly, getting made up to look like a woman in *Some Like It Hot*, was kind of a drag — in more ways than one."

JACK LEMMON to THE LEMON PIPERS:
"Well, I wouldn't say Walter Matthau was a bad housekeeper. Let's just say I went over to his place once and found several pieces of rotten fruit, a fly-blown pie, and a green tambourine."

VLADIMIR ILYICH LENIN to JOSEPH STALIN:
"So, it's settled. Hammer and sickle, Armand Hammer."

JOHN LENNON to DONNY OSMOND:
"What did I want to say to Linda McCartney the first time I saw her muck-amuck with Paul? 'Go away, little girl!' That's what."

JAY LENO to ARETHA FRANKLIN:
"If you and Trini Lopez get married, where would you live?"

LEONIDAS I to MAXWELL ANDERSON:
"I said, 'Sure we might reach Thermopylae. Sure, we might even hold off the Persians for awhile. For which we would possibly go down in the history books. But, what price glory?'"

LEVI (SON OF ALPHAEUS) to JEAN FRANCOIS LEPETIT:
"It's about these three guys and a baby…"

MERIWETHER LEWIS to THE MONKIES:
"I remember, we arrived at this pleasant valley, Sunday, and everyone was so exhausted we stayed the week."

LIBERACE to GEORGE BRUMMEL:
"Well, isn't that just dandy."

LIBERACE to EDGAR ALLEN POE:
"I remember just what he said. 'It'll be the perfect Christmas program. Just you, on that stage, with a piano and a bell, Lee.'"

ABRAHAM LINCOLN to PADDY CHAYEVSKY:
"You can't begin to imagine the altered states after the war."

THOMAS LIPTON to JACK NICKLAUS:
"Every tea can be important."

LITTLE MISS MUFFET to SADDAM HUSSEIN:
"Let me show you the way to gobble up those curds."

LITTLE MISS MUFFET to JIM STAFFORD:
"Everyone knows I'm deathly afraid of spiders, but few know I'm as equally afraid of snakes. Horrible things — spiders and snakes!"

LITTLE RED RIDINGHOOD to BETTE DAVIS:
"My, what big eyes you have!"

LITTLE RED RIDINGHOOD to JOHN DEAN:
"My, what a big mouth you have!"

LITTLE RED RIDINGHOOD to HERMAN HESSE:
"Oh, sure, I knew he was around somewhere. How? Well, for one, on the way to grandma's house, I step in wolf shit."

LITTLE RED RIDINGHOOD to KITTY KELLEY:
"My, what big eyes and ears and mouth you have."

HORACE LIVERIGHT to LIZA MINELLI, JAN AND DEAN:
"Bennett Cerf's city, no doubt about it, is New York, New York."

DAVE LOGGINS to KING GEORGE III:
"Now, if you really want a tea party, please, come to Boston."

KENNY LOGGINS to NENA, MICHAEL JACKSON, and DENIECE WILLIAMS:
"Well, it started out with possibilities for being one thriller of an evening. Lorna was there and released 99 Luft balloons. Then, Doctor Frankenstein introduced the monster with a rousing, 'Let's hear it for the boy!' However, when the creature came in, he had a foot loose, and things went downhill from there."

LOUIS (DUKE OF BURGUNDY) to GLADYS KNIGHT AND THE PIPS:
"I can say no more than that I heard it through the grapevine."

JOE LOUIS to HAM FISHER:
"He said, 'Joe, you're a palooka,' and I knocked him flat on his ass."

LOUIS XVI to JOSEPH GUILLOTIN:
"Give it a rest, or that thing will be the death of us."

LOUIS XVI to MARTY ROBBINS:
"'Don't worry, Marie,' I tell her. 'Everything is going to be all right. I promise.'"

BESSIE LOVE to THE SUPREMES:
"I don't know why, but every time I'd arrive at a party, everybody would go home."

BESSIE LOVE to GARY WRIGHT:
"Yes, I'd say I faded from sight, considering I have to begin every conversation these days with, 'Yes, by God, Love is alive!'"

LINDA LOVELACE to JIMMY DEAN:
"John Holmes? All we girls used to call him 'Big, Bad John.'"

LINDA LOVELACE to BOB FOSSE:
"What do I remember about *Deep Throat*? All that jazz, for one thing."

LINDA LOVELACE to BOB WOODWARD:
"Can't we talk about something besides Watergate for a change?"

ROB LOWE to GIOVANNI BOCCACCIO:
"She knew full well what she was getting into. Before we were even undressed, she asked, 'Is de camera on?' And I told her, 'Yes, de camera's on.'"

ROB LOWE to BEN HECHT:
"What do you mean, there's a part in it written just for me?"

ROB LOWE to LAWRENCE SANDERS:
"You think my video tapes are hot?! You should get a look at the ones Burt Reynolds took of Loni Anderson."

GEORGE LUCAS to DICK IRVING HYLAND, IAN MC LELLAN HUNTER:
"I don't know why you should think American graffiti the exception, rather than the rule. I was on Roman holiday recently, and *Kilroy Was Here!* was written all over the Coliseum."

GEORGE W. LUCAS to RONALD REAGAN:
"It's to do with space, and I'm thinking of calling it *Star Wars*."

JIM LUCAS to ANDREW LLOYD WEBBER:
"It's a hit!"

CHARLES LUCIANO to SIR WALTER SCOTT:
"Hell, I would rob Roy Rogers of everything he has, including Trigger, if given half the chance."

LUCIPHER to RICHARD MAIBAUM and CYRIL HUME:
"Oh, I'm called many things. Prince of Darkness, Satan, Fallen Angel, Old Jack, Old Nick, the Deceiver, Bad Man of Brimstone."

LUCIPHER to H.H. MUNRO:
"Sure, Hell has its hierarchy. We have our beasts and superbeasts, just like above-ground."

ARSENE LUPINE to MAURICE LEBLANC:
"God, yes, I've had adventures, but what about those of Barry MacKenzie, Bullwhip Griffin, Captain Africa, Captain Fabian, Captain Marvel, Casanova, Don Juan, Frank Merriwell, Gerard, Hajji Baba, Huckleberry Finn, Marco Polo, Mark Twain, Martin Eden, Red Ryder, Robin Hood, Robinson Crusoe, Sherlock Holmes, Sir Galahad, Smilin' Jack, Tartu, the Flying Cadets, the Wilderness Family, Tom Sawyer, Frank and Jesse James?"

MAB to EDMUND SPENCER:
"Three guesses who I am."

DOUGLAS MAC ARTHUR to ARNOLD SCHWARZENEGGER:
"I'll be back."

DOUGLAS MAC ARTHUR to DONNA SUMMER:
"I didn't make the dedication, but I sent a note, thanking them for naming the park after me."

ALI MAC GRAW to MILTON CANIFF:
"What can I tell you about Steve Mc Queen? I do remember this one time, he was piloting our plane, and I said, 'Steve, canyon at four o'clock.' And when he looked, he almost flew us into the side of a mountain. That the kind of stuff you want to hear?"

ALI MAC GRAW to THE MAMAS AND THE PAPAS:
"I remember once, we were in Montana, in the woods, and Steve took my hand and said, 'There's my very favorite creek, Ali, just up here, that I want you to see.'"

SHIRLEY MAC LAINE to MARCEL PROUST:
"Yes, I have this definite remembrance of things past."

SHIRLEY MAC LAINE to WOLFGANG PUCK:
"I'll be dining alone tonight, Wolfgang. So, that'll be a table for thirty-two, please."

SHIRLEY MAC LAINE to GERTRUDE STEIN:
"You only remember three lives? My dear, last count, I remember dozens."

SHIRLEY MAC LAINE to JOHN M. SYNGE:
"Maybe at one time. But now? Don't you think my brother is a little too old to rate, by anyone's standards, any title even similar to the *playboy of the western world*?"

SHIRLEY MAC LAINE to CATHERINE TURNEY:
"Well, once again, I'm back from the dead and happy to be here."

ROWLAND HUSSEY MACY to THE COMMOMDORES:
"I would have been at your performance for sure, but we had a sale on."

JAMES MADISON to JERRY HERMAN:
"Jerry, I'd like you to meet my wife."

MADONNA to FOREIGNER:
"Somehow, I want to get across that this guy makes this girl feel as if what he's doing feels like the first time. You know, like a virgin."

MADONNA to JOHN LENNON:
"Sorry, *Like a Virgin* has already been done."

MADONNA to RAY PARKER, JR.:
"Well, to tell you the truth, when he said, 'Let's go see Ghostbusters,' I thought I was going to Frederick's of Hollywood to check out a new line of invisible foundation garments."

MADONNA to THE MINDBENDERS:
"I said my marriage to Sean Penn was *love in a disastrous rut*. Naturally, the press misquoted me, saying I said it was *a groovy sort of love*."

MADONNA to THE STYLISTICS:
"Anyway you look at it, 'You make me feel like a virgin,' *is* the same as 'You make me feel brand new.' If you don't see that, I'm sorry."

FERDINAND MAGELLAN to THE BEACH BOYS:
"Yes, I confess, I get around."

FERDINAND MAGELLAN to VITUS BERING:
"Let's try and get this straight."

FERDINAND MAGELLAN to MAXINE NIGHTINGALE:
"I kid you not. Although we sailed always in the same direction, we ended up right back where we started from."

TOM MAGNUM to FLOYD MUTRUS:
"What would I have said to Robert and Rose Kennedy if they'd shown up at one of my shoots on the island? Gee, I don't know. 'Aloha, Bobby and Rose' maybe?"

NORMAN MAILER to ABBA:
"Damn right, tough guys don't dance. I know. Three times, I've seen a dancing queen. Elizabeth II with Prince Philip. Truman Capote with Tennessee Williams."

NORMAN MAILER to WILLIAM H. DANFORTH:
"Truman Capote and Tennessee Williams? Now, there are a couple of Twinkies."

RAY MALLAND to FRANK IFIELD:
"I may have been drunk through the whole lost weekend, but I remember you."

MAN IN THE IRON MASK to ENGELBERT HUMPERDINCK:
"Please, release me!"

DANIEL MANN to ROB LOWE:
"I want to talk to you about last night and about Mrs. Leslie."

JANE MANSFIELD to JANE AUSTEN:
"The parking attendant was genuinely rude, just because I didn't tip him. Can you imagine, he screamed out, 'Mansfield, park your own damned car!' at the very top of his lungs."

CHARLES MANSON to SISTER SLEDGE:
"I told them — 'We are family, and I'm the daddy. You do what I say, or else.'"

CHARLES MANSON to SLY AND THE FAMILY STONE:
"I'd have to agree, in any comparison between our two families, yours is more apt to come out looking like everyday people."

MARLA MAPLES to WALT DISNEY:
"So, I screamed — 'Donald, duck! Ivana has a vase.'"

MARLA MAPLES to OMAR SHARIF:
"Damn right, I've got trump."

JEAN-PAUL MARAT to THE SHIRELLES:
"Marie Antoinette is just a foolish little girl who I've never known yet to keep her head in a crisis situation."

FREDERIC MARCH to JULIUS CAESAR:
"Who said I'd be the death of you? Nostradamus? Jeane Dixon?"

CHRISTOPHER MARLOWE to FREDERICH VON SCHILLER:
"So I said, 'Come on, William, tell the truth. I wrote *Hamlet,* didn't I?'"

MARQUIS DE SADE to MICHAEL JACKSON:
"Beat it!"

MARY OF MAGDALA to OLIVIA NEWTON JOHN:
"So, I told Him right out, 'I'm hopelessly devoted to you.'"

MARY WHO HAD A LITTLE LAMB to THE FOUR SEASONS:
"So, I said to the officer in charge — 'I know who stole him. Her name is Shari Lewis. I know what she did with him, too. Made at least one lamb chop.'"

MASTERS AND JOHNSON to HALL AND OATES:
"Well, it's admittedly not perfect, but HUMAN SEXUAL RESPONSE is our attempt to define a method of modern love."

COTTON MATHER to ELI WHITNEY:
"Can't you think of anything but gin?"

JOHNNY MATHIS to DENIECE WILLIAMS:
"How about a song referencing John Holmes, Michelangelo's *David*, and Romeo?"

MARY C. McCALL to JOHN HOLMES:
"You have to be kidding! Really, it's *all* yours?!"

PAUL McCARTNEY to JOHN LENNON:
"My first reaction to your marriage, I'll admit, was, 'Oh, no!'"

PAUL McCARTNEY to STEVIE WONDER:
"I call it *Tropical Dicotyledonous Tree and Illegal Elephant Tooth*. Why don't you give a try at singing along?"

PAUL McCARTNEY AND WINGS to GUNS 'N' ROSES
"We saw tar. We saw feathers. We saw you headed out there. You trying to tell us what we witnessed wasn't a band on the run?"

JUNIE McCREE to MEL GIBSON:
"That's right! Put your arms around me, honey."

ED McMAHON to MARILYN MC COO and BILLY DAVIS, JR.:
"I tell them — 'You don't have to be a star to be in my show. Win, though, and you'll leave one.'"

FOWLER H. MEAR to JAMES MASON:
"Are you a Mason from the long line of Boston Masons?"

MEGA-DEATH to PAPER LACE:
"Did you go to that so-called concert by *Chicago*, Saturday night in the park? Did they die, or what? Real bummer!"

MENES to LONNIE MACK:
"I ruled Egypt for a good many years and founded my capital in Memphis. All you people know nowadays is Cairo."

SUE MENGERS to SHIRLEY ELLIS:
"I kid you not. He says, 'My name is Arnold Schwarzenegger,' and I'm, for sure, thinking he's playing some kind of name game."

MERLIN THE MAGICIAN to THOMAS MALORY:
"Say what you may in defense of Modred. Personally, I say he'll be the death of Arthur."

DAVID MERRICK TO J. ROBERT OPPENHEIMER:
"Sorry, Bob, but the way I see it, what you've got here is a real bomb."

DAVID MERRICK to THORNTON WILDER:
"I'd like to get you together with Dolly Levi and see if anything comes of it."

CHARLES E. MERRILL to MARQUIS DE SADE:
"You want stocks and bonds? I've got stocks and bonds."

CHARLES E. MERRILL to OSCAR WILDE:
"I'm sorry, but Hemingway's ego is way out of control. I finally told him he put far too much stock in the importance of being Ernest."

METHUSELAH to A.A. MILNE:
"I said to George Burns just the other day — 'Kids sure didn't act like they do today when we were very young.'"

MFSB to HENRY MILLER:
"Someone with dyslexia could misread that as, 'I'm so horny, I could fuck a tsop.'"

MICHELANGELO'S DAVID to LEVI STRAUSS:
"Pardon me, I could use some pants."

DAISY MILLER to MORGAN FREEMAN:
"You're driving this Daisy crazy!"

A.A. MILNE to KING C. GILETTE:
"Well, let me tell you the real reason I call him Winnie-the-Pooh."

LIZA MINELLI to JESSI COLTER:
"I'm not Lisa. My name is Liza."

LIZA MINELLI to THE COWSILLS:
"Well, New York, New York, to me, will always mean the rain, the park, and other things."

LIZA MINELLI to THE LOVIN' SPOONFUL:
"Yes, dears, I think you can safely say that these hundred-degree-New-York-New-York temperatures mean we are finally seeing summer in the city."

MISTER BLACKWELL to MARTHA JANE BURK:
"You're a walking calamity."

MOBY DICK to THE SUPREMES:
"Well, I told Ethel Waters — 'I suppose it's obvious my world is empty without you?!'"

MARILYN MONROE to MARCIE BLANE:
"Yes, I had an affair with Robert Kennedy. But to go so far as to call me *Bobby's girl* is, I think, quite absurd."

MARILYN MONROE to HOT CHOCOLATE:
"I'm tired of being thought of as some kind of inanimate sex object. Do you know that even John Kennedy took to calling me, *You sexy thing*?"

MARILYN MONROE to FRANCOIS RABELAIS:
"Men! Pant and drool. Pant and drool."

MARILYN MONROE to NEIL SESDAKA:
"At the time, I never dreamed anyone would make such a fuss over my being a calendar girl."

MARILYN MONROE to WILLIAM SHAKESPEARE:
"It was when I was married to Joe DiMaggio. We went to this big reception for the King of England. Afterwards, Joe asked me, 'Marilyn, did the King leer, or was I just imagining it?' I said, 'Joe, honey, you weren't imagining anything.'"

MARILYN MONROE to THE HOLLIES:
"It's called *Bus Stop*, based on a play by William Inge. I'll be starring in it with Don Murray, and the filming starts Monday."

CLAYTON MOORE to ELTON JOHN:
"Someone saved my life tonight. Who was that masked man?"

DOCTOR MOREAU to GEORGE BERNARD SHAW:
"It was a pygmy lion. The things Dr. Frankenstein does in his laboratory are truly amazing."

DOCTOR MOREAU to FRANK SINATRA:
"Dr. Frankenstein, genius in everything, always had a way with words. Do you know he introduced his monster to me as, *That's life!*?"

WILLIAM MORROW to BARBARA BUSH:
"Milli Vanilli? Don't we already have something on the bookstands by that dog?"

MOTHER OF MARTIN AND FRANK BEKINS to MARTIN and FRANK BEKINS:
"Get a move on!"

MOTHER OF MEL GIBSON to MEL GIBSON:
"Go outback and play."

MOTHER OF MICHAEL JACKSON to HER HUSBAND:
"Give me five!"

MOTHER OF HANNIBAL LECTER to HANNIBAL LECTER:
"How many times must I tell you to eat your cereal?"

MOTHER TERESA to SAMUEL RICHARDSON:
"You want virtue rewarded? Hollywood is *not* the place to go."

MOTHER TERESA to JOSEPH SMITH:
"I guess you could say that I, too, am a latter-day saint."

MR. HYDE to THE BEATLES:
"What is it with you? I feel fine. If you don't believe me, check with Dr. Jekyll."

MRS. MALAPROP to TOM JONES:
"So, Henny Youngman says to me, 'That's not my wife. She's a lady.'"

MRS. MALAPROP to SCHERAZADE:
"Little girls should be heard and not seen."

PATRICIA MULLENS to HAL:
"Speak for yourself!"

ROBERT MURDOCH to CHARLES SCHNEE:
"I'd rather you to give me a script that can convince Leroy Brown and Jaclyn Smith it's right for them."

ARTHUR MURRAY to HOWARD DIETZ:
"So when we had that brown-out awhile back, Kathryn and I kept right on dancing in the dark."

ARTHUR MURRAY to VACHAL LINDSAY:
"As far as dances go, I think you'll quite enjoy the conga."

ARTHUR MURRAY to DONNA SUMMER:
"May I have the last dance?"

KATHYRN MURRAY to JACQUES COUSTEAU:
"Although Valentino went far with the tango, you've talent to go even farther with the calypso."

KATHYRN MURRAY to LEO SAYER:
"The very first time I met Arthur, he walked up to me at this party and said, 'You make me feel like dancing.'"

N

MARTINA NAVRATILOVA to WILLIAM M. HOUGH and F.R. ADAMS:
"I do find myself wondering who's kissing her now."

MARTINA NAVRATILOVA to D.H. LAWRENCE:
"I agree with Sappho: there's nothing wrong with women in love."

MARTINA NAVRATILOVA to THE EVERLY BROTHERS:
"First I loved men. Then, I loved women and men. Finally, though, I said, 'Bye bi-love,' and now I love just women."

GUNNAR NELSON to STANLEY SHAPIRO:
"Matthew and I toyed with the name *Carbon Copy,* but we figured that would apply better if we were black."

GUNNAR NELSON to THE SEEKERS:
"This chick hangs onto me, like glue, and she tells me, 'I'll never find another you.' About then, in walks Matthew."

PRINCE ROGERS NELSON to WILLIAM MAKEPEACE THACKERY:
"As a singer? *Vanity*? Fair."

PRINCE ROGERS NELSON to THE CARS:
"Well, to be quite frank, when the guys screamed, 'Let's go crazy and see *The Cars,*' I figured they meant a drive or something."

WILLY NELSON to HENRY D. SEYMOUR:
"I think it's about time you and I gave those poor endangered gators aid."

NERO to JOE HAYDEN:
"There's going to be a hot time in the old town tonight."

ISAAC NEWTON to HENRY H. WILLIAMS:
"Then the theory of gravity hit me. Right there, in the shade of the old apple tree."

OLIVA NEWTON-JOHN to MILTON SNAVELY HERSHEY:
"My mother always warned me not to accept candy from strangers. That said, introduce yourself, because I want that candy bar. Please, mister, please."

OLIVA NEWTON-JOHN to JOHN HOLMES:
"No way did you have to ask the good Lord for a little more, Love, did you?"

JACK NICHOLSON to PAUL MC CARTNEY AND WINGS:
"'Drive,' he said. What could I do but listen to what the man said? I drove him all of the way to Chinatown."

RICHARD MILHOUS NIXON to BEETHOVEN:
"In retrospect, I suppose the break-in of Watergate was dumb dumb dumb … dumb."

RICHARD MILHOUS NIXON to DICKIE GOODMAN:
"John Dean's mouth is so big, I took to calling it *Mr. Jaws* after just a few hours of its blabbermouth testimony."

RICHARD MILHOUS NIXON to THE O'JAYS:
"Martha Mitchell and John Dean? Back-stabbers, the both of them!"

RICHARD MILHOUS NIXON to THE SPINNERS:
"So, Bob Woodward told me, 'You've covered your ass pretty well on this, Dickie, but, slowly and surely, I'm working my way back to you.' The nosey bastard was good as his word."

ALFRED BERNHARD NOBEL to DR. RALPH BUNCHE:
"Damn if this isn't a first!"

PHILIP NOLAN to THOMAS WOLFE:
"I can't go home again."

JOHN W. NORDSTROM to THE CAPTAIN AND TENNILLE:
After *the customer is always right*, my motto has always been *shop around, people, shop around*."

OLLIE NORTH to THOMAS JEFFERSON:
"I ran contra- to what?"

OLLIE NORTH to FRANK SINATRA:
"I did it my way."

NOSTRADAMUS to JIMMIE ANGEL:
"I see you headed for a big fall."

NOSTRADAMUS to ROBERT CHAMBERS:
"I predict your name will eventually be linked with pot."

NOSTRADAMUS to THE GEORGE WASHINGTON:
"I see a sandwich."

SINEAD O'CONNOR to JAMES BALDWIN:
"I'm the one without hair, James, so why is everyone calling you *bald one*?"

SCARLETT O'HARA to WILLIAM INGE:
"So, I said to the darkie at the top of the stairs, 'You get right down here and start over again until I can see my face in this banister.'"

SCARLETT O'HARA to OSAMA BIN LADEN:
"I surely do love Tara."

O. HENRY to CHARLES A. PAGE:
"What the world needs now is a candy bar named after me."

ROSIE O'NEILL to NEIL DIAMOND:
"When Julia Child removed the lard, she scooped up the residue and asked, 'How about some delicious cracklin', Rosie?'"

ANNIE OAKLEY to JOHN DENVER:
"*I'm an old cowhand, good as any man. My idea of fun is to shoot a gun.* Think you've got what it takes, boy, to put that into music for me?"

JOHN OATES to DARYL HALL:
"If you leave me, there'll be no more haulin' oats."

ODYSSEUS to ELZIE C. SEGAR:
"So, the Cyclops had us trapped, see. And I figured if I could find a spear, a stick, or something else sharp, to like *pop-eye* the bastard, we might be home free."

OEDIPUS to SIGMUND FREUD:
"My problem is complex."

OLD MAN (AND THE SEA) to SAMUEL TAYLOR COLERIDGE:
"I went to sea to get a fish, and I can truthfully say I got my wish. But before I got my fish aboard, a giant shark did fully gorge."

OLD OWL (WISE) to RONALD REAGAN:
"Who?"

OLD SCRATCH to STEVIE WONDER:
"I've always found superstition a useful tool."

OLD WOMAN (WHO LIVED IN A SHOE) to CLYDE BEATTY:
"Sometimes, it's a three-ring circus around here."

OLD WOMAN (WHO LIVED IN A SHOE) to JEAN COCTEAU:
"Do you think infants terrible? Well, admittedly, sometimes I don't know if I'm coming or going."

OLD WOMAN (WHO LIVED IN A SHOE) to DION:
"And these three are Abraham, Martin, and John."

OLD WOMAN (WHO LIVED IN A SHOE) to HERMAN MELVILLE:
"Herman, this is Moby, Dick, Billy, Bud..."

OLD WOMAN (WHO LIVED IN A SHOE) to BILLY PRESTON:
"Truthfully, I was outa space long before I was outa children."

OLD WOMAN (WHO LIVED IN A SHOE) to ALEX RAYMOND:
"Finally, I had to find something to keep all the little ones occupied. So, I broke down and bought a Junglegym."

JOHNNY OLSEN to WILLARD MOTLEY:
"Go ahead. Knock on any door."

OPHELIA to MIKHAIL BULGAKOV:
"You know, they're calling Hamlet *The Great Dane*. Well-fitted, if you ask me. The man has *the heart of a dog*!"

ROY ORBISON to JULIA ROBERTS:
"Oh, pretty woman, can you please give me directions to Rodeo Drive?"

GEORGE ORWELL to ERIC BURDON:
"I'm sure, Mr. Burdon, that you do, indeed, believe your many fans would be interested in your purchase of a farm. However, I see that as more a press release than material for a novel."

GEORGE ORWELL to ZAGER AND EVANS:
"Yes, I can see where you might find my book *Nineteen Eighty-Four* seemingly dated. If I'd had better sense, I would have set it in the year 2525."

OSMONDS to TOM SMOTHERS:
"The song's *Yo-yo*, man."

WILLIAM PALEY to ARNOLD SCHWARZENNEGGER:
"Linda Hamilton? Terminate her, too."

PETER PAN to C.C. BECK:
"The crocodile may have gotten his hand, but with his new hook, the captain is a marvel."

DOLLY PARTON to KENNY ROGERS:
"Well, we've proved that you don't need me for a hit, and I don't need you for one, but this song sounds just right for the two of us. So, what do you say?"

MINNIE PEARL to HIROHITO:
"You obviously have me confused with someone else. On December 7th, at the time in question, I was in my arbor, not getting bombed, as you insinuate."

SAM PECKINPAH to HARRY REEMS:
"I'm afraid that's a typo. What this movie calls for is another *six*-shooter."

SEAN PENN to ANDREA DEL SARTO:
"Go ahead and paint my ex-wife. You can call it *Madonna of the Harpies*."

JOE PENNY to THE BEATLES:
"I could hardly believe it. I mean, a street named after me in my old hometown. Actually, I guess it's more of a lane, but it's pretty much the same thing, right?"

SERGEANT PEPPER to ALAN HOPGOOD, HENRY EDWARDS, THE BEATLES, AND PRINCE ROGERS NELSON:
"You really think I can use these two guys — Alvin Purple and Claude Rains — for my *Lonely Hearts Club Band*? Purple! Rains! Come over here and let's hear you play something."

PERSEPHONE to ARTHUR RIMBAUD:
"That's right. Then I spend the other half of the year with my mother."

PHANTOM OF THE OPERA to LINDA RONSTADT:
"Why did I abduct her? Quite frankly, I just woke up one morning and asked myself. 'When will I be loved?' I figured that day was as good as any to make it happen."

HOLLY MICHELLE PHILLIPS to JOHN BERRY:
"Mama Cass, bah! I was the best singer of that group."

PABLO PICASSO to ADOPLH HITLER:
"Say, I stopped off at that little bar in Guernica last night and got bombed."

ALLAN PINKERTON to FRANK BUCK:
"Sometimes I do luck out and bring 'em back alive."

PINOCCHIO to CYRANO DE BERGERAC:
"Might I suggest that to succeed you put your nose to the grindstone?"

PINOCCHIO to JOE DOWELL:
"Just because I have a wooden heart doesn't mean I can't fall in love."

PLASTIC SURGEON to MICHAEL JACKSON:
"By all means, don't stop 'til you get enough."

ABE PLOUGH to THE CARPENTERS:
"I hate rainy days and Mondays. Mainly, rainy days."

EDGAR ALLAN POE TO PINK FLOYD:
"My favorite? Possibly *The Cask of Amontillado*. When Fortunato screams up a storm, but the narrator calmly mortars one after another brick in the wall."

EDGAR ALLAN POE to STEVE PERRY:
"In *The Cask of Amontillado*, you mean? Oh, sherry was Fortunato's downfall. No doubt about it."

EDGAR ALLAN POE to BARBRA STREISAND:
"If nothing else, Dr. Frankenstein is doggedly persistent. Finally, I had to come right out, in no uncertain terms, and tell him the *Tell-Tale Heart* is *my heart* and *belongs to* me."

EDGAR ALLAN POE to BONNIE TYLER:
"The *Tell-Tale Heart*? It's a heartache story all right."

MARCO POLO to RICK NELSON:
"Travelin', man. It gets in your veins, if you know what I mean."

IACOPO CARRUCCI PONTORMO to JAMES JOYCE:
"I wanted to do a portrait of myself, the artist as a young man, so to speak, and that's just what I did."

POPE JOHN PAUL II to HARRY BROWN:
"In a word — purgatory."

POPE JOHN PAUL II to CHUBBY CHECKER:
"As I don't believe there are rocks in limbo, it would be purely conjecture to say any such rock would be called a *limbo rock*."

POPE JOHN PAUL II to GEORGE LUCAS:
"R-2; D-2; and we have a *Bingo* by the little lady over in the corner!"

POPE JOHN PAUL II to THE DOORS:
"Real gutsy dame, that Saint Joan. She was tied to a stake but still had the ability to challenge her persecutors to 'Light my fire!'"

POPE JOHN PAUL II to DIONNE WARWICK:
"Frequently, I say a little prayer during the course of any given day."

POPPIN FAMILY to WILLIAM H. BONNEY:
"You goin' to go straight? You goin' to stay a gunman? Which way you goin', Billy?"

PORKY PIG to JAN CHRISTIAAN SMUTS:
"You're a real bore, you know that?"

COLE PORTER to FRANCIS THE MULE:
"I get a kick out of you."

EMILY POST to EDNA FERBER:
"Dinner at eight sounds great."

EMILY POST to JACK (THE KNIFE):
"How many times must I tell you to use a fork?"

EMILY POST TO LULU and THE BOXTOPS:
"Well, the correct form of address for a knight is *sir*. But to address the letter *to sir with love*, might be going it a bit far."

EMILY POST to JOHN D. ROCKEFELLER:
"If you ever want to be respected, it's important you establish a standard for others."

ELVIS PRESLEY to OLD NICK:
"I know you! You're the Devil in disguise."

VICTORIA PRINCIPAL to KENNY NOLAN:
"I told the producers, 'Of all the alternatives to getting Patrick Duffy back into the story-line, I like dreamin' the best.'"

PROMETHEUS to THELMA HOUSTON:
"Oh, I know what Zeus wanted when he chained me to these rocks. He wanted me to beg, 'Please, don't leave me this way!' Needles to say, I won't give him that satisfaction."

J. ALFRED PRUFROCK to T.S. ELIOT:
"Sing? Of course I can sing. How about I sing my rendition of *Love is a Many Splendored Thing*?"

WOLFGANG PUCK to JEREMY LLOYD and DAVID CROFT:
"So, I said, 'Pardon me madam, are you being served?' It was Xaveria Hollander, do you believe?"

WOLFGANG PUCK to OGDEN NASH:
"Michael Jackson always asks to be seated in the private dining room."

WOLFGANG PUCK to ALFRED LORD TENNYSON:
"Yes, I'd say it was a very good day, starting off with the whole *Light Brigade* coming in and ordering an eight-course dinner, with wine, then charging the total, with large tip, on their VISA card."

WOLFGANG PUCK to CHAIM TOPOL:
"If you'll play the fiddle for your meal, it's on the house."

JOSEPH PULITZER to GWENDOLYN BROOKS:
"Well, if you don't take the prize!"

QUASIMODO to ARGENT:
"Dr. Ruth Westheimer's advice? 'Quasimodo, you'll have a better chance with women if you try harder to hold up your head.'"

QUASIMODO to MISS MARPLE:
"I've this hunch."

QUASIMODO to GILBERT O'SULLIVAN:
"I just got tired of night after night, going to bed alone, again, naturally."

QUASIMODO to ANITA WARD:
"You want to ring my bell? Go head."

DAN QUAYLE to RALPH ELLISON:
"I might as well be an invisible man for all the attention people pay me."

QUEEN ELIZABETH II to MICHAEL JACKSON:
"I never thought of it, but, yes, I suppose some people do find *Big Ben* phallic."

QUEEN ELIZABETH II to FERENC MOLNAR:
"Call the guards, man! Call the guards."

QUEEN ELIZABETH II to STEVIE WONDER:
"So, I tapped John Wayne on the shoulder with my sword and said, 'Arise, Sir Duke!'"

QUEEN ISABELLA I to PHILIP ROTH:
"I stood right here, on this very parapet, waved my hanky, and yelled, 'Goodbye Columbus!'"

QUEEN MUM to CRISPIAN ST. PETERS:
"So, I whispered to Elizabeth — 'The piper is so pied, he can't even blow a proper *Danny Boy*.'"

CATALYTIC QUOTES 105

QUEEN OF SHEBA to HUMPHREY BOGART:
"You tell Geraldine that the only real African Queen is this one, and she'd better not forget it."

ANTHONY QUINN to FRANKIE VALLI:
"Three guesses where we filmed *Zorba the Greek*."

R

R2D2 to THE JACKSON FIVE:
"Even if you programmed me to tango, waltz, cha-cha, swing, rumba, mashed potatoes, and any other dance, I would still be more than a mere dancing machine."

CLAUDE RAINS to ENGLAND DAN and JOHN FORD COLEY:
"Yes, I really did once tell Virginia Bruce, 'I'd really love to see you tonight.'"

RAMPUNZEL to JAMES RADO, GEROME RAGNI, and GALT MC DERMOT:
"Hair? Here's hair!"

ALEX RAYMOND to CHARLES GEORGE GORDON:
"Hold on! I'll be there in a flash, Gordon!"

NANCY REAGAN to MELISSA MANCHESTER:
"You think what Kitty Kelley wrote about me is bad, you should hear how she talks about you."

RON REAGAN to SHAUN CASSIDY:
"I don't remember mine as a necessarily literate family. The first few years of my life, about the only thing either of my parents said to me was, 'Da Doo, Ron, Ron!' as they followed me around the house with a pooper scooper."

RONALD REAGAN to ERNIE BUSHMILLER:
"I want Nancy! I want Nancy! I want Nancy!"

RONALD REAGAN to SPRING BYINGTON:
"Accidents will happen, according to Mrs. Hoyle."

RONALD REAGAN to O. HENRY:
"Margaret Thatcher? I say that the present state of the English economy is, to a large extent, the gift of the Maggie."

RED BARON to BILLY WILDER:
"I was hunting in Africa and fell into this hole someone dug for lions. More than a few American flyers came to wish I had never climbed out."

ORVILLE REDENBACHER to ALAN ORMSBY:
"Now *I* know popcorn!"

ROBERT REDFORD to DAN HILL:
"Sometimes when we touch, usually when I'm on horseback, it's downright electric."

HARRY REEMS to BOB WOODWARD:
"What do I remember about *Deep Throat*? For one, always being on the other end of the stick."

ERICH MARIA REMARQUE to SIMON AND GARFUNKEL:
"All quiet on the western front!"

BURT REYNOLDS to LOU CHRISTIE:
"White lightnin' strikes you dead if you're not damned careful how you go about making it."

BURT REYNOLDS to JOHN FRED AND HIS PLAYBOY BAND:
"My divorce from Judy Carne? Well, she took it harder than I did. For days after, I'd turn around and find Judy in disguise, with glasses, following me everywhere."

DEBBIE REYNOLDS to CONNIE FRANCIS:
"What did I feel when Eddie ran off with Liz? Well, I guess everybody's somebody's fool, at one time or another."

LUCY RICARDO to KENNY ROGERS:
"My friends call me *Lucy*. You can call me *Lucille*."

LIONEL RICHIE to MICHAEL JACKSON:
"I believe Billie Jean King is the best female tennis player — truly."

LIONEL RICHIE to DIANA ROSS:
"I think you and I should make endless love. What do you think?"

HARRY RICHMAN to TACO:
"My favorite movie? *Puttin' on the Ritz*. I had a great time during shooting."

CHARLES F. RICHTER to CAROLE KING:
"It's too late! I feel the earth move!"

RIGHTEOUS BROTHERS to PIERRE ABELARD:
"Brother Abelard, something tells us that you've lost that lovin' feelin'."

JOAN RIVERS to WALTER BRENNAN:
"I think it hurt the most when right there on national, night-time television, Johnny called me *Old* Rivers."

ROAD RUNNER to THE PLAYMATES:
"Beep! Beep!"

JULIA ROBERTS to WALLACE SMITH:
"I account the fact that I almost married not once but several times, to the immature way I was always falling in love with co-stars."

ORAL ROBERTS to BOB SEGER AND THE SILVER BULLET BAND:
"And I say, shame, shame, on the moon flashed by Kevin Costner in *Dances with Wolves*, by Mel Gibson in *Lethal Weapon*, by Richard Gere in *American Gigolo*. And shame to all the other pants-dropping actors who corrupt the morals of today's youth."

JOHN D. ROCKEFELLER to THE ASSOCIATION:
"Would you believe that when I told the doctor I had gas, he thought I meant *Standard Oil*? I finally had to say that I was *windy* to get my point across."

JOHN D. ROCKEFELLER to THE RASPBERRIES:
"You're not apt to get anything done, to anyone's satisfaction if you're not prepared to go all the way."

ROY ROGERS to JOHN SUNUNU:
"Get a horse!"

ROY ROGERS to TRIGGER:
"Get stuffed!"

ROMEO to VAL GUEST:
"That's obviously another man's poison. I used all of mine. If you don't believe me, ask Juliet."

ROOFTOP SINGERS to SIGMUND FREUD:
"So, every time we did it, she'd say, 'How many times must I tell you not to walk right in on mommy and daddy, in our room, without first knocking and waiting for one of us to say you can come in?'"

FRANKLIN DELANO ROOSEVELT to GEORGE BAKER:
"Churchill finally came right out and said, 'That Hitler is one sad sack of shit!' Of course, we all concurred."

AXL ROSE to EDMUND WILSON:
"If I want a castle, by God, I'll have one!"

PETE ROSE to JAMES FORD BELL:
"You play right, you play to win. Right?

PETE ROSE to PAT BOONE:
"So, you haven't had a hit in years. Ain't that a shame?"

PETE ROSE to GLORIA GAYNOR:
"I know there are people who think old Pete is down and out, but I will survive. I'll bet on it."

PETE ROSE to DOLLY PARTON:
"God knows, I never gamble, but I'll give you 9-to-5 that those 2 aren't naturals."

DIANA ROSS to WARREN BEATTY:
"You want to do what while we're upside-down?"

KEVIN ROWLAND to EILEEN BRENNAN:
"Come on, Eileen, I'm telling you how it is. Fall in love with Michael Jackson, and he's going to tell you to beat it."

RICHARD RUARK to MIKHAIL BULGAKOV:
"Well, you know how much I admired Hemingway and refused to believe he was a lush. Well, I went down to Mexico last month to learn something of value from the master. And, margarita in hand, he was obviously three sheets to the wind and had been for quite sometime."

ANN RULE to THE CREEDENCE CLEARWATER REVIVAL:
"Yes, I suppose I could give you the known specifics of the Green River murders, but I'd prefer you get them from my book."

RUMPELSTILTSKIN to BLOOD, SWEAT, AND TEARS:
"So, I gave the bitch the straw and the spinning wheel and told her to see if she could spin any gold without me."

KEITH PALMER RUSSELL to RICHARD ADAMS:
"The rabbit definitely died."

KEN RUSSEL to THE ANGELS:
"There's this film festival for oldies-but-goodies in Seattle, and they're planning to show my *The Boy Friend*."

KURT VON VOGEL RUSSELL to OTTO HARBACH:
"Filming *Backdraft* is okay, except all the smoke gets in your eyes."

WARD RUSSELL to MARK TWAIN:
"Tom Cruise and Nicole Kidman? What can I say? Tom saw her, and that was that."

BABE RUTH to MARQUIS DE SADE:
"You know? The feeling I get, whenever I make a really solid hit, is almost sexual."

S.O.S. BAND to THE BEATLES:
"You want help, then take your time in sending your *Mayday*."

CARL SAGAN to MITCHELL PARISH:
"Literally billions and billions of particles from stars — star dust — fill the universe."

CARL SAGAN to HAJI HASSANAL BOLKIAH MU'IZZADIN WADDAULAH:
"Billions, and billions, and billions…"

SAINT GEORGE to UPTON SINCLAIR:
"Did you get a look at that old dragon's teeth?"

EVA MARIE SAINT to GEORGE BERNARD SHAW:
"You know that I told Miss Joan Fontaine? 'You're dealing with Eva Marie Saint, Joan, and don't you forget it.'"

EVA MARIE SAINT to MOTHER TERESA:
"Don't give me any of your holier-than-thou bullshit!"

KYU SAKAMOTO to A TASTE OF HONEY:
"So what that I was really cooking with sukiyaki? You know the consumer — filled up one moment, hungry the next."

RICHARD SALE to LEIGH VANCE:
"'It's all happening,' I told Mary Loos. 'Let's do it again.'"

ANTONIO SALIERI to MARGARET MITCHELL:
"I tried my best. Really I did. 'Mozart,' I said, 'do something for strings. You're good with strings.' So, what's he done? He's gone with the winds and come up with this horrible opera *The Magic Flute*."

SAMSON to JULIA ROBERTS:
"The truth is: I, too, have been sleeping with the enemy."

GEORGE SAND to **WILLIAM BOWERS**:
"You want me to help you with an alias? How about Jesse James, Jimmy Valentine, Mary Dow, Nick Beal, the Deacon, or the Doctor?"

COLONEL HARLAND SANDERS to **JOHN FOWLES**:
"You and yours are chicken!"

SANTA CLAUS to **MAXWELL ANDERSON**:
"I remember, this one winter set in at the Pole with real vengeance, and it was really hell getting out of there for Christmas deliveries."

SANTA CLAUS to **CAESAR CHAVEZ**:
"Ho, ho, ho!"

SANTA CLAUS to **SAM M. LEWIS and JOE YOUNG**:
"I'm sitting on top of the world."

SANTA CLAUS to **THE FOUR SEASONS**:
"Snow. Sleet. Temperatures below zero. Power outages. Someone shot my reindeer. Thirty-five gifts to the wrong households. 25 December 1963? Oh, what a night!"

DAVID SARNOFF to **THE SWEET**:
"Our intention, here at NBC, is to put that upstart network FOX on the run."

VIDAL SASSON to **PRINCE CHARLES**:
"What I said was that you were at that age where you could use as good *dye*."

TELLY SAVALAS to **SINEAD O'CONNOR**:
"Who loves your hair, baby!"

TOM SAWYER to **BOB HOMEL**:
"Werewolf!"

LEO SAYER to **THELMA HOUSTON**:
"When I need you, don't leave me this way."

JOSEPH M. SCHENCK to ERNIE BRADFORD:
"I'm looking for something decidedly high-brow, like about Edmund Burke; combined with a bit of humor, a la Bugs Bunny."

ROY SCHERER, JR. to SIMON AND GARFUNKEL:
"You can rely on me. I won't let you down. I am a rock."

VICTOR SCHONFELD to THE ANIMALS:
"So you want me to make your film."

CHARLES SCHULZ to THE COASTERS:
"A little bald boy, see. Bashful. A real klutz. Never gets the girl."

CHARLES SCHULZ to THE ROYAL GUARDSMEN:
"It's a little hard to explain the how, until I've drawn up a few strips in example, but I plan to have Snoopy don flying apparel and give battle to the Red Baron."

CHARLES SCHWAB to MANUEL BENITEZ:
"I'm talking a killing in a bullish market."

ARNOLD SCHWARZENEGGER to ARCHIE BELL AND THE DRELLS:
"I can tell, just by looking, that what we've go here are a lot of pecs, lats, and abdominals that we need to tighten up."

ARNOLD SCHWARZENEGGER to R.B. GREAVES:
"You want to talk women's lib? You should have seen my wife's face the first time I told her, 'Take a letter, Maria.'"

ARNOLD SCHWARZENEGGER to SAMANTHA SANG:
I tried out the Strasberg school of acting, but Lee kept insisting I show more emotion than I could ever muster."

ARNOLD SCHWARZENEGGER to THE T-BONES and THE BEATLES:
"No matter what shape your stomach's in, we can work it out together."

NORMAN SCHWARZKOPF to NEIL SEDAKA:
"Yes, I think it would be safe to say that there was bad blood between George Bush and Saddam Hussein."

NORMAN SCHWARZKOPF to THE BEE GEES:
"What it all boiled down to, there in the sands of Iraq, was stayin' alive."

WILLARD SCOTT to JOHN BURKE:
"Granted, it may rain cats and dogs. But pennies from heaven? No way!"

WILLARD SCOTT to BETTY COMDEN and ADOLPH GREEN:
"My philosophy has been that it's always fair weather somewhere."

WILLARD SCOTT to ALBERT HAMMOND:
"It never rains in southern California — but that it pours."

WILLARD SCOTT to THE RIGHTEOUS BROTHERS:
"Today, we have an ebb tide scheduled for two-forty-five p.m."

NEIL SEDAKA to PETER GABRIEL:
"So, you live right next door? Do you know this is the first time I've ever lived next door to an angel?"

GEORGE SEGAL to THE OHIO PLAYERS:
"Love *Rollercoaster*! Probably my best movie, ever."

MICHAEL SEMBELLO to DONNA SUMMER:
"I agree that Oprah Winfrey is a maniac, as far as her job is concerned. No doubt that she works hard for the money."

WILLIAM SHAKESPEARE to LEONARD BERNSTEIN:
"I don't usually discuss works-in-progress, but I've this plot about a young man and a young woman — star-crossed lovers, as you would — who…"

WILLIAM SHAKESPEARE to ELIZABETH BARRET BROWNING:
"I told Pedro Alvarez Cabral and Gaspar Corte-Real, 'You want to impress me, send me sonnets.'"

WILLIAM SHAKESPEARE to LANGSTON HUGHES:
"Do you believe he wanted our road show of *Hamlet* to stop in Harlem? Would you believe I told him we would?"

OMAR SHARIF to H.M. WALKER:
"Seems like all through the shooting of *Dr. Zhivago*, we worked in temperatures below zero."

GEORGE BERNARD SHAW to CLARK KENT:
"Man, and super, man!"

TOMMY SHAW to ARNOLD SCHWARZENNEGER:
"Hey, man, in *Terminator*, and *Terminator 2*, I thought your *Mr. Roboto* act was super."

PATRICK SHEEHY to WINGS:
"At an early age, I had Jeane Dixon tell me that with a little luck, I could possibly get a lucky strike and make my name in lights."

MARY WOLLSTONECRAFT SHELLEY to THE EDGAR WINTER GROUP:
"Yes, well, I've heard your song, and I've a notion to slap you with a suit for blatant plagiarism."

ROGER SHERMAN to MARY WOLLSTONECRAFT SHELLEY:
"Well, it was just after we'd declared independence. Some of us were celebrating at the Ol' Ale House. We were having a really good time, too, until Thomas Jefferson, drunk as a skunk, came up, grabbed my drink out of my hand, and screams, 'What in the hell are you doing, using Ben Franklin's stein?'"

ROBERT SHERWOOD to NATHAN BEDFORD FORREST:
"We should get together and look up the Earl of Huntington."

BROOK SHIELDS to LINDA RONSTADT:
"You knew, of course, that the movie was originally set in Louisiana and called *Blue Bayou*. There was some kind of production trouble that involved the Florida Film Commission, so Randal Kleiser transferred shooting to a lagoon in the Pacific."

DINAH SHORE to GENERAL ROBERT H. BARROW:
"I'm afraid you have my family confused with the Shores of Tripoli."

CARLY SIMON to WILLIAM DE VANE:
"Take my word for it. I said nothing whatsoever about you in any song."

NEIL SIMON to CHICAGO:
"Every Saturday, in the park, I used to go barefoot."

PAUL SIMON to NEIL SEDAKA:
"Art and I have been together for a good many years, and breaking up is hard to do."

PAUL SIMON to THE 1910 FRUITGUM COMPANY:
"Let me tell you what I say."

PAUL SIMON to JOHN WAITE:
"For years, I called and wrote Art, trying to get across the I'm-missing-you-let's-try-and-get-back-on-track message to him. Finally, it was make it on my own or sink trying."

RICHARD SIMON to STENDHAL:
"Think Sitting Bull and Martin Luther King, Jr."

RICHARD SIMON to EVELYN WAUGH:
"We agree, then, that Shelly Winter's reminiscences about her childhood, *Maidenhead Revisited,* really don't have the right degree of *oomph* and should be returned to her for change of title and rewrite?"

THEODORE SIMONSON to WILLIAM WRIGLEY, JR.:
"Leave it to you to gum up the works."

WALLIS SIMPSON to RICHARD RODGERS:
"I can't help it. I keep thinking about the king and I."

ISAAC M. SINGER to BETSY ROSS:
"So what?"

SITTING BULL to JOHNNY CASH:
"I tell you, I am, too, Sioux."

SITTING BULL to JORGEN INGMANN:
"Where was George Custer coming from? I'll tell you. From nowhere. Up to the very end, he thought I was an Apache."

SITTING BULL to LARRY VERNE:
"I kid you not. He said to me, 'My name is George Armstrong Custer, but you can call me Mr. Custer.' Well, let me tell you what I thought about that."

RED SKELTON to GARY LEWIS AND THE PLAYBOYS:
"Ask your father, Gary, and I'm sure he'll back me up on this, since it's been his and my experience that just about everybody loves a clown."

LIZ SMITH to MR. ACKER BILK:
"That's no stranger on the shore. That's Burt Reynolds."

LIZ SMITH to BOZ SCAGGS:
"I told Ivana if she wanted the world to know how it felt to be dumped on by Mr. Donald Trump, all she had to do was give me the lowdown."

SUSAN SMOTHERS to HARRIET BEECHER STOWE:
"Every summer, we used to all hop in the car and head off to Uncle Tom's cabin."

TOM SMOTHERS to JOHNNY THUNDER:
"Now, this trick with the yo-yo — watch carefully — is called the *loop-de-loop*."

GALE SONDERGAARD to THE SUPREMES:
"I sometimes dream that I have David Hedison back in my arms again."

GALE SONDERGAARD to FRANKIE VALLI:
"I finally came right out and told Jeff Goldblum — 'I can't take my eyes off of you.'"

GALE SONDERGAARD to VAN HALEN and DURAN DURAN:
"I confess, I wanted to see hoity-toity Little Miss Muffet jump. So, I sneaked up. And, I sat down beside her. The reflex of that girl something to see, let me tell you."

DAVID SOUL to THE SUPREME BEING:
"Don't give up on us."

JOHN L.B. SOULE to CHRISTOPHER COLUMBUS:
"Go West, young man, go West."

ANN SOUTHERN to GLEN CAMPBELL:
"Why ever would it concern you as to how I spend my nights?"

SPARTACUS to SADDAM HUSSEIN:
"We who are about to die, salute you."

SPARTACUS to NAT TURNER:
"Maybe you ought to try it my way."

LEON SPINKS to JIMMY JONES:
"A lot of people said it was just luck that let me win that championship fight with Ali. Just between you, me, and the gatepost, I won because of good timin'."

SYLVESTER STALLONE to JACKIE WILSON:
"So, I said to John Travolta — 'I don't want you looking like a wimp if we're to keep it stayin' alive for this movie. So, you're going to work out with me. And I'm not talking baby workout, either."

PHILIP STANHOPE to SINCLAIR LEWIS:
"My opinion of William Dodd, after he forged my name to cover his extravagances? Dodd's worth less than the rope it'll take to hang him."

BARBARA STANWYCK to GEORGE BERNARD SHAW:
"He says, 'As far as a power in this town, I'm major, Barbara. You want to go places, I can help you. Let's talk over there on my casting couch.'"

BARBARA STANWYCK to THE GREG KIHN BAND:
"I don't know. John Sturges says the script is just right for me. Seems my husband falls off a jetty, gets stuck under a waterlogged timber, while I seek help from a convicted criminal. Does that sound like something that would play in Peoria?"

EDWARD STAPLETON to KAREN DE WOLF and DWIGHT V. BABCOCK:
"You'd think if I could have expected nothing else, it would have been for someone to bury me dead, wouldn't you? Well, guess again!"

BRENDA STARR to THE TORNADOES:
"You know what they say — 'Telephone, telegraph, tell Starr.'"

RINGO STARR to JOHN LENNON:
"You want to marry Yoko Ono? I say, do whatever gets you through the night."

RINGO STARR to DOCTOR RUTH WESTHEIMER:
"It don't come easy."

ROBERT STARR to JEANE DIXON:
"My sign? Leo, Virgo, Libra, Scorpio, Sagittarius, Capricorn, Aquarius, and Pisces."

MARY STEENBURGEN to CYNDI LAUPER:
"God, no, it isn't a sex movie. It's about Jack the Ripper escaping Victorian London for modern San Francisco in an H.G. Wells' time machine."

GLORIA STEINEM to JOHN STEINBECK:
"You asked, so I'll tell you. In my opinion, the world would be a far better place if depleted of a larger number of mice and men."

JOHN B. STETSON to S/SGT BARRY SADLER:
"Let me sing you this tale of green berets, colored hats that have seen far better days. They used to grace every artist's head, although, depending, they might be red, or black, or blue, or aquamarine; although nowadays people don't like to be seen in any kind of hat at all, exposing heads to all manner of fall — be it rain, or hail, or driving sleet, or snow that, likewise, soaks the feet."

JAMES STEWART to TOMMY ROE:
"Funny thing, but throughout the whole filming of *Vertigo*, I was dizzy."

ROD STEWART to NIKITA S. KHRUSHCEV:
"I haven't forgotten so much that I still can't do a good job of burying you."

HARRIET BEECHER STOWE to HARRY HARRISON KNOLL:
"I don't know. It just was always very easy to visualize Uncle Tom's cabin in the cotton."

JOHANN STRAUSS to KAY STARR:
"Sure, I like jazz. Sure, I like rap. Sure, I like rock and roll. Waltz, though, is what I prefer."

STREETWALKER to PROMETHEUS:
"Hey, handsome, got a light?"

BARBRA STREISAND to JAMES FORD BELL:
"So, how come your company makes *Gold Medal*, but you don't bring me flours?"

BARBRA STREISAND to D.H. LAWRENCE:
"Woman in love. Woman in love."

ROBERT STROUD to HUDSON HAWK:
"I'm afraid you'll never fly."

ROBERT STROUD to GEORGE WESTINGHOUSE:
"Give me a break!"

SUCCUBUS to BOBBY DARIN:
"Honey, I'm just what you're looking for."

SUETONIUS to ANDREA DORIA:
"No doubt in my mind that you'll go down in history."

SULEIMAN I to HUDSON HAWK:
"Let's talk turkey."

DONNA SUMMER to JOHN TRAVOLTA and OLIVIA NEWTON-JOHN:
"My nights are my own. So, I'd appreciate you leaving me to them."

SUPERMAN to NEIL ARMSTRONG:
"Up, up, and away!"

SUPERMAN to BILL CONTI:
"It seems like every time I get together with Lois Lane, something always comes up that I have to tell her, 'Gonna fly now.'"

SUPREME BEING to JOHN A. MURPHY:
"Let there be light!"

KIEFER SUTHERLAND to KATHRYN SCOLA, EDITH SKOURAS, and NEIL SIMON:
"With Julia Roberts, it's always good-bye. Girl, either one of you might know the why, but this guy doesn't."

SWEET to THE COMMODORES:
"What do you mean, you heard that we were having orgies on the road, the groupies calling them *Sweet Love*?"

TARZAN to W.R. BURNETT:
"You know, until I got a look at all the asphalt in New York City, I thought mine was the only jungle."

TARZAN to GIUSEPPE DI LAMPEDUSA:
"I'm glad you asked, because I've actually always preferred the leopard to the lion."

TARZAN to ISAK DINESEN:
"I told Jane that if we kept getting harassed by film crews and tourists, we're going to pack up and move out of Africa, bag and baggage."

TARZAN to JEAN-BERNARD-LEON FOUCAULT:
"Now, you've got the swing of it."

TARZAN to DR. WILLIAM A. HINTON:
"And if you're really methodical, and put your mind to it, you might even luck out and see the spiraling parakeets."

TARZAN TO UPTON SINCLAIR:
"I tell you, this place is the jungle."

ELIZABETH TAYLOR to THE BEE GEES:
"Richard Burton? I can only ask you what I asked him after our second-time around went as belly-up. 'How could love so right continually go so wrong?'"

ELIZABETH TAYLOR to FATS DOMINO:
"I'm in love again."

ELIZABETH TAYLOR to HALL AND OATES:
"A banana split? Look guys, I can't go for that. No can do. I'm svelte again, and I goddamn intend to stay that way — this time."

ELIZABETH TAYLOR to CLAUDE LELOUCH:
"I looked at all my marriages as another man, another chance."

ELIZABETH TAYLOR to LTD:
"Yes, in Richard Burton's case, we were both back in love again."

ELIZABETH TAYLOR to BOBBY VEE:
"I was flattered, but I had to tell him, 'Rodney Allen Rippy, it's best you come back when you grow up.'"

JAMES TAYLOR to LOLLY MADONNA:
"How sweet it is to be loved by you."

EDWARD TEACH to K.C. AND THE SUNSHINE BAND:
"Sure, I'll tell you how it is being a pirate. Not nearly as glamorous as you might imagine. Nine times out of ten, it's a case of getting drunk on your ass and dancing around, making a bloody fool of yourself, while you shake, shake, shake, shake your booty."

GWENDOLEN TERASKI to CORNELIUS RYAN:
"If you ask me, any bridge to the sun is a bridge too far."

TERI DE SARIO to K.C., and THE CAPTAIN AND TENNILLE:
"Yes, I'm ready. Do that to me one more time."

THE BEATLES to HEDDA HOPPER:
"We promised not to tell, but do you want to know a secret?"

THE BEE GEES to DAVID BOWIE and MICK JAGGER:
"In this video, see, you should be dancing in the streets."

THE BEE GEES to TED KNIGHT:
"You've definitely got a fever. The question is, can we do anything about it?"

THE BYRDS to THE DAVE CLARK FIVE:
"Turn! Turn! Turn! Over and over."

THIS LITTLE PIGGY to THE IMPALAS:
"I wanted to go to market; I would have settled to stay home. I would have liked some bread and butter, but I would have settled for none. But, for the life of me, I'm sorry I ran all the way home."

HENRY DAVID THOREAU to GRETA GARBO:
"I want to be alone."

HENRY DAVID THOREAU to IVAN TURGENEV:
"What you need is a month in the country. From personal experience, I know it'll do you wonders."

THREE DOG NIGHT to MARY TODD LINCOLN:
"Sorry, Mrs. Lincoln, but it's tradition that the show must go on."

THREE LITTLE PIGS to EDWARD ALBEE:
"Who's afraid of the big bad wolf?"

THREE LITTLE PIGS to JACK LONDON:
"You think we're kidding? Look out there. See wolf?"

MEL TILLIS to VLADIMIR NABOKOV:
"H-h-how about a c-c-character n-n-named Humbert Humbert?"

RIP TORN to MARY MAC GREGOR:
"I suppose I was somewhat of a Lothario. I remember once, I had this thing going with two lovers, each of whom grabbed me in a restaurant and commenced a tug-of-war that almost left me drawn and quartered."

P.J. TOWLE to JOHN LLOYD WRIGHT:
"What do I think of when you say, 'Abe Lincoln'? Logs. He used to chop them. Log cabin. Abe had one, as you very well know."

JOHN TRAVOLTA to OLIVIA NEWTON-JOHN:
"You're the one that I want."

LEE TREVINO to IRVING CAESAR:
"So, Jack Nicklaus and I, just the two of us, mind you, teed off at Pebble Beach."

RICHARD TREVITHICK to LITTLE EVA:
"It's called a locomotive. And when it moves, it's called locomotion."

DONALD TRUMP to DOROTHY FIELDS:
"I can't give you anything but love, baby. Ivana depleted me of my cold cash."

DONALD TRUMP to MOSS HART:
"I said, 'Ivana, I had this money when you married me. When we divorce, you can't take it with you.'"

IVANA TRUMP to JAMES M. BARRIE:
"How did I know? It's what every woman knows — when her husband cheats on her."

IVANA TRUMP to JIMMY CHARLES:
"The chances of Donald and me ever getting back together again? I'd give you a million to one."

IVANA TRUMP to IRVING KAHAL:
"So I said, 'Donald, you want to play dirty, then I'll be seeing you in court.'"

IVANA TRUMP to CARSON MC CULLERS:
"So, I said to Marla, 'You have to be kidding! No way would I consider being a member of the wedding.'"

IVANA TRUMP to JOHNNY TILLOTSON:
"Finally, I'd had so much, I picked up this book of poetry and threw it at him."

TOMMY TUTONE to JENNY LIND:
"Eight, six, seven, five, three, oh, nine. Jenny, can you add those for me?"

TWEETIE BIRD to FREDERICK LONSDALE:
"Yes, canaries sometimes sing. Do they have us confused with ostriches or what?"

TWIGGY to PETER PAUL RUBENS:
"What do you mean, I'll never make it big as a model?"

OLIVER TWIST to ANDY WARHOL:
"More sir. I want more. I'm still hungry."

MIKE TYSON to CYNDI LAUPER:
"Let me tell you how it is for me in a relationship with any woman. She love me and treat me nice, I do the same by her. She bop me, I bop her. It's simple as that."

MIKE TYSON to THE CAPTAIN AND TENNILLE:
"I'm an easy-going guy, right. But she was on my back all the time. Finally, I told her, 'Do that to me one more time, and it's lights out for you, Baby.'"

U

UNCLE SAM to DWIGHT D. EISENHOWER:
"I want you."

UNCLE SAM to RUFUS:
"Okay, you don't have to pay any income tax this year."

VINCENT VAN GOGH to ELVIS PRESLEY:
"What did she do with my ear after I mailed it to her? She sent it back, the unappreciative bitch! Marked the package, *Return to Sender*."

RIP VAN WINKLE to RAYMOND CHANDLER:
"I really think readers, especially in the medical profession, would enjoy the details of my big sleep. Unfortunately, I'm not a writer."

RIP VAN WINKLE to HARVEY FIRESTONE:
"You want to see tired?"

RIP VAN WINKLE to CHARLES HALL:
"Give it a rest!"

GLORIA VANDERBILT to HALL AND OATES:
"It might be easy for some, but for me, it was never easy being a rich girl."

BOBBY VEE to SIGMUND FREUD:
"I can't help it. Every time I try to — you know? — do *it*, I get this feeling I'm being watched. It's as if the night has a thousand eyes, every one of which is watching my efforts to perform."

BOB VILA to TRINI LOPEZ:
"I could show you how to fix that fast enough if I had a hammer."

BOB VILA to NOAH:
"For an ark, I'd recommend 2x2s."

LEOPOLD VON SACHER-MASOCH to PEDRO ARONDONDO:
"Hit me!"

LEOPOLD VON SACHER-MASOCH to BORDEN CHASE:
"Take it from someone who knows. You can get whipped on the ass, on your arms, on your legs, even on the soles of your feet. But nothing beats a good old-fashioned backlash."

LEOPOLD VON SACHER-MASOCH to CHER:
"Let the beat go on."

LEOPOLD VON SACHER-MASOCH to JAMES FENIMORE COOPER:
"Here's a tale to tell, of me stripped down to nothing more than leather stockings, and she with her cat-o'-nine-tails."

LEOPOLD VON SACHER-MASOCH to JOHN COUGAR and THE CAPTAIN AND TENNILLE:
"Hurts so good. Do that to me one more time, please."

LEOPOLD VON SACHER-MASOCH to ROBERT FROST:
"You want switches to deliver the most exquisite pain? Cut them from birches."

LEOPOLD VON SACHER-MASOCH to JAMES L. KRAFT:
"I always knew if I got together with the Marquis de Sade, we'd have the makings of a dream whip."

LEOPOLD VON SACHER-MASOCH to LOBO:
"I know exactly what I want to say to the Marquis de Sade. 'I'd love you to want me.'"

LEOPOLD VON SACHER-MASOCH to PAUL REVERE AND THE RAIDERS:
"I can really get my kicks out of kicks. You might try them yourself sometime."

LEOPOLD VON SACHER-MASOCH to ELVIS PRESLEY:
"I suppose it sounds like an oxymoron, but it really is oh-so good when I feel so bad."

LEOPOLD VON SACHER-MASOCH to IRVING STONE:
"Oh, yes, let me tell you about the agony and the ecstasy."

BARBARA WALTERS to JIM PALMER:
"What kind of tree would you be?"

DIONNE WARWICK to PLASTICMAN:
"I can tell you one thing that isn't two: I'll never love this way again."

GEORGE WASHINGTON to ANATOLE FRANCE:
"What did I say when my mother caught me reading that filth? I cannot tell a lie, now, nor could I tell one, then. I told her it was a friend's book."

GEORGE WASHINGTON to JULIAN MITCHELL:
"You may think that we, in the colonies, and you, in England, have a lot in common, but you'll soon find out that we, over here, are entirely another country."

GEORGE WASHINGTON to OLIVIA NEWTON-JOHN:
"I cannot tell a lie. I honestly love you."

GEORGE WASHINGTON to NOAH WEBSTER:
"I give you my word."

LEW WASSERMAN to RON TURBEVILLE:
"What kind of movie would I like? Think Buster Crabbe and Billie Jean King."

JOHN WAYNE to MILES STANDISH:
"Hey, pilgrim."

DENNIS WEAVER to GARY WRIGHT:
"I should have never told Sigmund Freud about my recurring dream. Whenever we cross paths, he insists, 'Tell me about your dream, Weaver.'"

NOAH WEBSTER to FRANZ KAFKA:
"How do you ever expect to write about America if you can't even spell it?"

NOAH WEBSTER to HERMAN MELVILLE:
"How do you expect to write a book about Indians when you can't even correctly spell tepee?"

JOSIAH WEDGEWOOD to NELLIE MELBA:
"You are one sweet dish!"

ERICH WEISS to FLORENZ ZIEGFELD:
"Not only can I change into Harry Houdini, but I can perform that magic every single night."

LAWRENCE WELK to LON BARRY:
"A one … and a two … and a three."

LAWRENCE WELK to MARTHA AND THE VANDELLAS:
"North Dakota. July 6, 1936. Temperature one-twenty-one degrees. Now, that was a heat wave."

ORSON WELLES to THE TEMPTATIONS:
"Yes, Oprah Winfrey wanted a kiss. Even asked for one. Unfortunately, I had to tell her what should have been obvious — 'Oprah, you can't get next to me; I can't get next to you; that's just the law of physics.'"

MAE WEST to ROD STEWART:
"Do ya think I'm sexy? Yes? Well, then, why don't you come up and see me sometime?"

ROLAND WEST to LESLIE HISCOTT:
"I have an alibi. You have an alibi. What about Brian Desmond Hurst?"

DOCTOR RUTH WESTHEIMER to AIR SUPPLY:
"Personally, I don't like *impotent*. Better is *all out of love*."

DOCTOR RUTH WESTHEIMER to JEWEL AKENS:
"Yes, it's true. I finally got the *Old Woman Who Lived in a Shoe* to confess that her mother got the bit all wrong about the birds and the bees."

DOCTOR RUTH WESTHEIMER to HERB ALPERT:
"On today's program, we're going to discuss how to get a rise, and we have Julia Child here with us to give us the ups and downs of yeasts."

DOCTOR RUTH WESTHEIMER to B.T. EXPRESS:
"You say to do it 'til *you*'re satisfied. I say to do it 'til you're *both* satisfied."

DOCTOR RUTH WESTHEIMER to JOHANN BACH:
"It's perfectly okay to play with your organ."

DOCTOR RUTH WESTHEIMER to ERIC CARMEN:
"So, you're tired of staying home and doing it — how do you say? — 'All by myself.'"

DOCTOR RUTH WESTHEIMER to DAVE CORTEZ:
"The planned subject of my TV show tonight will be *The Happy Organ*."

DOCTOR RUTH WESTHEIMER to FOREIGNER:
"You want to know what love is. I want to know what love is. I'm sure, we *all* would like to know what love is. I'm afraid there's no pat answer."

DOCTOR RUTH WESTHEIMER to JOE FRANK and HAMILTON REYNOLDS:
"Yes, there is still a school of thought that says, 'Don't pull your love.' However, I don't prescribe to that archaic way of thinking."

DOCTOR RUTH WESTHEMIER to GLADYS KNIGHT AND THE PIPS:
"You think my life is one perfect sexual experience after another? Get real! I've got to use my imagination, too."

DOCTOR RUTH WESTHEIMER to LINDA RONSTADT:
"The problem is that people think it's so easy. In reality, it isn't easy at all, even when it's hard — if you catch my drift."

DOCTOR RUTH WESTHEIMER to JOHN SHODER:
"What you do alone in the dark is no one's business but your own."

DOCTOR RUTH WESTHEIMER to PAUL SIMON:
"So I told Abelard — 'If you're not going to piss, get off the pot. Even I can think of at least fifty ways to leave your lover.'"

DOCTOR RUTH WESTHEIMER to BILLY SWAN:
"You have a sexual problem? Ask Dr. Ruth. Chances are good that I can help."

DOCTOR RUTH WESTHEIMER to THE BEATLES:
"You got it right. Come together is best. But it's not always possible. So, don't think you're the exceptions if you don't manage it every time."

DOCTOR RUTH WESTHEIMER to THE BELLAMY BROTHERS:
"To put it short and simple, a vasectomy is an operation performed so as not to let your love flow, while, simultaneously, not inhibiting performance or sexual enjoyment."

DOCTOR RUTH WESTHEIMER to THE SWEET:
"I told Mr. Nelson — 'There's nothing wrong with being little, Willy. It's what you do with it that counts.'"

JAMES WHALE to ALEKSANDR PUSHKIN:
"So, he said, 'How about Karloff for the role of the monster in *Frankenstein*?' And, I said, 'Boris's good enough for me.'"

OSCAR WILDE to HALL BARTLETT:
"All the young men? You must be joking! I never knew the names of half of them."

OSCAR WILDE to BROOK BENTON:
"So, I told him — 'Truman Capote. You may pretend to be hard to get, but it's just a matter of time.'"

OSCAR WILDE to GLEN CAMPBELL:
"You a cowboy? Honey, rhinestone, maybe."

OSCAR WILDE to JANICE ELLIOTT:
"So I said to him — 'I've heard of the daisy chain, but what in the hell is the buttercup chain?'"

OSCAR WILDE to CONNIE FRANCIS:
"Come on, Connie. You can tell me where the boys are."

OSCAR WILDE to MARVIN GAYE:
"What do you mean your name is a misnomer? Let's get it on!"

OSCAR WILDE to ADOLPHUS GREEN:
"I left as soon as Truman Capote started to disrobe, and Norman Mailer started yelling, 'Will you look at that fruit strip?!'"

OSCAR WILDE to MINOR C. KEITH:
"We fruit have to unite."

OSCAR WILDE to JACK LONDON:
"Jack! Jack! Jack!"

OSCAR WILDE to HENRY MYERS:
"Well, I'd have to say the prize for the black room goes to either the one had by Leopold von Sacher-Masoch or the one had by the Marquis de Sade."

OSCAR WILDE to RICK SPRINGFIELD:
"Your mother is one-hundred percent: Don't talk to strangers. In the meantime, let me introduce myself and Mr. Truman Capote."

OSCAR WILDE to THE BREAD:
"I've always wanted to make it with bread."

OSCAR WILDE to THE PLATTERS:
"Rock Hudson? Played the great pretender to the last, didn't he?"

OSCAR WILDE to THE VILLAGE PEOPLE:
"For a good time, I recommend the showers at the Y.M.C.A."

OSCAR WILDE to ADAM WADE:
"Well, there's this loo off Trafalgar Square. I used to go there regularly and get dates from the writing on the wall."

OSCAR WILDE to EDGAR WALLACE and ERLE STANLEY GARDNER:
"Oh, I hired Perry Mason, all right, but he was telling everyone mine was 'the case of the frightened lady.' I needed someone to show me a bit more respect."

ROBIN WILLIAMS to TOMMY SANDS:
"Know what you get when you crowd all the dancers from *American Bandstand* into one phone booth?"

FLIP WILSON to FAUST:
"The Devil made me do it!"

OPRAH WINFREY to AGATHA CHRISTIE:
"Well, there were two-hundred cookies; I ate one-hundred-ninety. And, then, there were ten. I ate six. And, then, there were four. I ate three. And, then, there was one. Finally, I ate that …"

OPRAH WINFREY to TENNESSEE ERNIE FORD:
"You heard me right. I went on that much publicized water diet and lost sixteen tons."

SHELLEY WINTERS to ISAK DINESEN:
"And everybody's damned right! My tale does deserve to be told."

WITCH OF ENDOR to THE MONKEES:
"A tiny dash of bat's wing. A tiny dash of dragon's tooth. A small dose of newt's tongue. A small dose of snake's scale. A little bit of you. A little bit of me."

WITCH OF ENDOR to SANTANA:
"Some people see a witch only as some kind of black-magic woman. Actually, we're so very much more than just that."

WITCH OF ENDOR to THE SEARCHERS:
"So, I said to Warren Beatty — 'Here it is, but remember, please, that you're now up to love potion number nine, and I only have ten available.'"

WITCH OF ENDOR to THE STEVE MILLER BAND:
"Look, boys, try to get serious. There's more to this than abracadabra."

THOMAS WOLFE to JOHN DENVER:
"Take it from someone who knows. You can't go back home again."

NATALIE WOOD to ROBERT BUNSEN:
"Sometimes you really burn me up."

NATALIE WOOD to TINA TURNER:
"When Warren Beatty said to me, cool as you please, 'What's love got to do with it?', I knew exactly what was in the relationship for me."

TAMMY WYNETTE to ARETHA FRANKLIN:
"So, I finally just spelled it out for him. 'You give me some R-E-S-P-E-C-T, George Jones, or I want a D-I-V-O-R-C-E.'"

BORIS YELTSIN to OGDEN NASH:
"You want hard-line? Well, I don't think you're going to find any harder than those drawn by Lenin."

ANGUS YOUNG to SHIRLEY JACKSON:
"What do you mean, my generation never learned to count? Twenty-four, sixteen, two, twelve, nine. Or spell? A,C,D,C."

BRIGHAM YOUNG to ELVIS PRESLEY:
"Know what Barbara Walters asked me? 'Are you lonesome tonight?' She had to be kidding, right?"

FELIX YUSSOUPOV to BRUCE WILLIS:
"Talk about die hard."

(z)

FINIS

ABOUT THE AUTHOR

William Maltese was born in the Pacific Northwest. He has a B.A. in Marketing/Advertising and spent an honorable tour of duty in the U.S. Army, achieving the rank of E-5.

He started his authorial career writing for the men's pulp magazines and has since penned more than 150 books, both fiction and nonfiction. According to queerhorror.com, this included the first gay werewolf novel ever published. He also has written a number of bestselling women's romances under the name "Willa Lambert" for houses such as Harlequin and Carousel, including the internationally acclaimed Harlequin SuperRomance #2 (*Love's Emerald Flame*), which is being reprinted by the Borgo Press imprint of Wildside Press along with many of his other novels.

He encourages his fans to visit his websites:

www.williammaltese.com
www.myspace.com/williammaltese
www.myspace.com/draqual
http://www.myspace.com/maltesecandlegallery

www.ingramcontent.com/pod-product-compliance
Lightning Source LLC
LaVergne TN
LVHW011203080426
835508LV00007B/581